FOR CHARLIE HINES —
GREAT BALLPLAYER, GOOD FRIEND. AND
ONE CATCHER I WOULD NEVER TRY TO
RUN ON!   SEE YOU ON THE FIELD.
Joe

A Short Season
with Ernie

A Memoir

Joe Seme

Joe Seme

Library of Congress Control Number: 2021919257
ISBN: 978-1-63062-032-5 (paperback)
ISBN: 978-1-63062-033-2 (e-book)
Printed in the United States of America
Cover and Interior Design: Christy King Meares

For information about this title or to order books and/or electronic media, contact the publisher:

simply francis publishing company
P.O. Box 329, Wrightsville Beach, NC 28480
www.simplyfrancispublishing.com
simplyfrancispublishing@gmail.com

Dedication

For Deb, Tracy, and Sam. I wish you
had been part of this. In so many
ways, you are.

Author's Note

This book is my personal memoir and all of the events depicted are pretty much the way they happened, or at least the way I remember them. Some of the characters' names have been changed, as have one or two names of places, but most are intact. Conversations may not be "word for word" accurate, but they are close. I have been carrying this book in my head, and more importantly in my heart, for more than sixty years.

I apologize for the condition of some of the photos, letters and clippings, since many are close to or more than a hundred years old and quite fragile, carefully lifted from my grandmother's scrapbook. Without it, this book would not have been possible.

Joe Seme

TABLE OF CONTENTS

Prologue

Picture this, if you will: A man in his early fifties; a dignified, small of stature quiet man with a wonderful sense of humor, full of fun. He is a husband, father, former professional ballplayer, and something of a celebrity in his home city. Picture also a teenage son who is not only a gifted athlete like his father but also a brilliant student with unlimited horizons. There is also a younger daughter who idolizes her brother, Joe. Their mother is a tough-minded, practical woman who guards her children like a mama bear.

Life is fine for this family in the mid-1930s. The man has a great job with a growing company. He plays golf and attends a lot of baseball games at Shibe Park, later re-named Connie Mack Stadium. They have a comfortable home in a quiet neighborhood of row houses in Philadelphia. Juniata Park is at the end of their street. Their sights are set on a small summer cottage that they can fix up, somewhere along the New Jersey coast, perhaps near Wildwood or Ocean City. Both towns were favorite vacation destinations for folks from Philly, at least for those who could afford the luxury while trying to beat the summer heat of the city. As they said back then and I know they still say in that inimitable Philly accent, "We're 'gawn' down the shore." Hopefully, it will be soon after Joe gets a scholarship. The former ballplayer likes to go fishing and crabbing, or simply sitting under an umbrella with a cold one. One of these days ....

And then every family's worst nightmare takes place. Joe dies after a freak accident, and like every other family that is faced with dealing with the loss of a child, their world is turned upside down. The tough-minded, practical mother retreats into the bottle. The retired ballplayer/father retreats into himself. The younger daughter is simply a lost soul. A gaping black hole opens up in each of their hearts.

Fast forward ten years. The daughter is now happily married and gives birth to a son, the first grandson of a distraught man and the tough-minded, practical mother. Cracks in the walls of the dark rooms begin to appear and sunlight filters in. Maybe, just maybe, there is life ahead.

The Rarest Play in Baseball

In late September of 1923, a twenty-four-year-old shortstop named Ernie "Red" Padgett was called up from the Memphis Chicks of the Southern Association to the parent club Boston Braves of the National League. Ernie had closed out the minor league season with a .317 batting average in 122 games, and was among the league leaders in stolen bases. The Braves were impressed also with his fine defense, his baseball instincts, quickness, and strong throwing arm. The "September Call-Up," even today, gives minor leaguers who have had solid seasons a chance to experience life in "The Show." For many, it's a short-lived experience, but two or three weeks they will never forget. For the lucky ones, it can be the beginning of a dream life in baseball. Ernie was one of the lucky ones.

His first at-bat for the Braves that autumn was a less than eventful, late-inning pinch hitting appearance on October 3rd against the Brooklyn Robins. He grounded out. Nonetheless, Braves manager Fred Mitchell decided to start Ernie in the last three games of the season. He played second base and collected his first major league hit on October 4th against the Phillies in a 10 to 2 loss. The next day (Friday) was an off day, and the season was scheduled to end on Saturday, October 6th, with a doubleheader against the Phillies. It should be noted here that both the Braves and the Phillies had atrocious records in 1923. It was a bad year all the way around for Boston fans because the cross-town American League Red

Sox finished in the cellar with a record of 61 and 91; 37 games behind the pennant-winning Yankees. The Braves were even worse, with a record of 54 and 100; 42 games out of first place. The Braves were two games up on the Phillies on the last day of the season, but a sweep of the doubleheader by the Phillies would have resulted in a tie for last place, so a more-or-less meaningless doubleheader became important to the Braves and their remaining faithful fans.

The *Boston Globe* noted that, "The weather was cold and with an overcast sky most of the time." Ed Cunningham, a veteran *Boston Herald* sportswriter, wrote "there were about 1000 frost-bitten customers in attendance." The dismal crowd was representative of the Braves' season, but those fans in attendance got their money's worth in the first game alone as the game was tied going into the bottom of the 14th inning. The Braves won the game 5 to 4 on an RBI triple by first-baseman John "Stuffy" McInnis. Ernie Padgett, playing shortstop for the first time, had a walk, scored a run, and participated in three double plays. Due to the lengthy first game, approaching darkness and the day growing colder by the minute, the managers agreed that the second game would last only five innings. After winning the first game, Braves manager Mitchell was now assured of avoiding the cellar so he decided to rest his regulars in the second game. Ernie started the game again at shortstop. On the mound for the Braves for his first and only start in the big leagues was rookie lefthander Joe Batchelder.

By the third inning, the Braves were leading 4 to 1, which would end up being the final score. In the top of the fourth inning James "Cotton" Tierney led off with a single to left. Cliff Lee then followed up with a single to right field. Walter Holke then came to the plate representing the potential tying run. On the first pitch, Holke ripped a low line drive to the shortstop side of second base with both runners taking off on the pitch. Ernie broke toward second base, snared the line drive for the first out, stepped on second to retire Tierney who was racing toward third, and ran down Cliff Lee before he could retreat to first. According to the *Boston Globe*:

"Without faltering an instant in his stride, Padgett set his sights on Lee, coming down from first. The startled runner attempted a quick retreat but Padgett ran him down in a couple of strides, applying the tag, killing the Quaker rally." The entire play took less than ten seconds. The game was then halted because of darkness, but since the home team was ahead at the time, it was declared an official game, keeping the record of Ernie Padgett's feat intact. As Casey Stengel, Ernie's teammate in 1924, who later became the legendary manager of the Yankees and Mets, and life-long friend used to say, "You could look it up." This was the first unassisted triple play recorded in the National League.

Ironically, "Cotton" Tierney was traded by the Phillies to the Braves for the 1924 season (and traded away by the Braves at the end of the season). Tierney and Ernie, having 'gotten close' in the middle of Ernie's triple play, became teammates and friends for one season. Players in those days were simply 'property,' which was made clear in the contracts. They were bought, sold, or traded on the whims of management. There was no such thing as free agency and players had almost no bargaining power.

TRIPLE PLAY

Ernie Padgett, former Memphis second baseman, playing shortstop for the Boston Braves Saturday, entered the baseball hall of fame when he made an unassisted triple play during the second game of the Boston-Philadelphia double - header. Here's how Padgett made it:

Tierney and Lee had singled and were on second and first, respectively. Holke lined to Padgett, who ran to second, retiring Tierney and then caught and tagged Lee before he could get back to first.

ERNIE PADGETT

Ernie's triple play was not the only instance of a miraculous defensive feat in Boston's 1923 baseball season. Three weeks earlier, first baseman George Burns of the Red Sox pulled off an unassisted triple play against the Cleveland Indians in a 12-inning game at Fenway Park. But as Paul Shannon, sportswriter for the *Boston Sunday Post* pointed out, "Burns was a seasoned veteran with a wealth of experience and perhaps might have had similar chances in his big-league career before, but Padgett, a raw recruit, was entitled to even more credit for showing the quickness of thought and the lightning execution that this play required."

Ernie Padgett was my grandfather. Although he died at the age of fifty-eight in a VA Hospital in 1957, he is still, and always will be my hero. As a kid, I would have done anything to please him so when he decided that he (with a lot of encouragement from my father, a fine athlete himself) would turn me into a ball player, I happily went along with it.

When I was five-years-old he was making me jump to catch the ball and throwing short hops at my feet or to my backhand side. At the time, I couldn't understand why a former major leaguer couldn't throw it to me so I could catch it more easily. Later, as a high school infielder, second baseman on the Marine Corps Air Station Yuma baseball team, and even now as an old guy still playing a young man's game, I appreciated, and still appreciate the ease with which I can backhand a hard grounder in the hole. I mentally thank Ernie every time.

He played five seasons in the majors and in truth, according to some modern assessments of his statistics, for whatever reason, possibly several injuries along the way, he never lived up to his potential. However, he had a nice career. He had the usual stops along the way, beginning with grammar school and sandlot baseball teams, on up through semi-pro, minor leagues and ultimately the majors. This book is a sort of homage to Ernie and a fond look back at my *way* too short season with him, growing up with Pop Pop, as we called him, and the way he taught me to not only play the game the right way, but to develop a passion for the game that for me has never waned.

When I tell my friends that I would rather play baseball than anything else, they often suggest 'something else' that might be more pleasurable. "Yes," I tell them. "But a baseball game can last for three or four hours. And you don't necessarily fall asleep soon afterward!"

The Early Years & A Quirk of Fate

Ernie was born on March 1, 1899, in Philadelphia and died on April 15, 1957, at age fifty-eight after a long battle with lung and colon cancer, thanks in part to a couple of packs of unfiltered Camels a day and the lack of medical technology that exists today. He grew up in the Port Richmond section of Philly and at age ten he played the infield for the Taylor School, his first experience in organized baseball. That's Ernie at age ten; front row; far left.

Ernie continued to play baseball and was also a stand-out soccer player. After high school, he and his older brother Ralph played for a couple of semi-pro teams in the uptown section of the city. My 'great uncle' Ralph was eight years older than Ernie and was a highly-touted, tough hard-hitting outfielder and sometime catcher with a very strong throwing arm who was considered a sure bet to end up in the majors. Ernie, at the time, was considered to be an average infielder, possessing good speed and a strong arm. Unlike Ralph, who was a power-hitter, Ernie was a slap hitter who hit to all fields and showed only occasional power, and was an excellent base stealer.

Both brothers were on their way to careers in baseball, until Kaiser Wilhelm and The Great War put those careers on hold. Ernie and Ralph enlisted in the Army in 1917 and both went to France, Ralph as an infantryman and Ernie with Battery 'C', 108th Artillery Regiment.

Ernie saw limited action. I'm sorry to say I don't know anything about Ralph's service. I do know that by 1919 they were both playing for the Nativity Athletic Club of Port Richmond, Philadelphia, semi-pro baseball team, having picked up where they left off, two years older, and now Army veterans.

A quirk of fate landed Ernie in professional baseball while Ralph played nearly his entire career on semi-pro diamonds. Eventually, Ralph gave up baseball and concentrated on working and raising a family. As a kid, I remember Ernie and "Uncle Ralph" sitting in the backyard of Ralph's home in Pine Beach, New Jersey, drinking a beer and talking baseball. Most of the time, they were listening to a Phillies game on the radio, sometimes tossing a ball back and forth while I played in a muddy creek by the back fence and chased frogs.

Sometimes Ernie would include me in the game of catch to show Uncle Ralph how well I could catch for four or maybe five years old. All I remember about Uncle Ralph is that he was bald and his wife Frances had a terrific but scratchy Fu-Manchu mustache. Ernie had lots of reddish hair and his sister Ethel had flaming red hair. Even as a little kid I recognized that she must have been something special when she was young. Back then, I didn't realize Uncle Ralph had been a ballplayer. He just seemed to be old and grumpy.

The Quirk of Fate

A man named Joe O'Rourke lived in the Port Richmond area of Philly and he paid close attention to the semi-pro baseball activity in the city. In 1919 he also happened to be the manager of the Charlotte Hornets of the South Atlantic League (also called the "Sally" League, which would be equivalent to today's Class AA minor leagues). Joe paid special attention to the Padgett brothers before they went into the military, and even more so now that they were back from the war with no obligations. They became good friends, sharing their enthusiasm for baseball.

As it turned out, the Charlotte Hornets needed a third baseman for the 1919 season, so Joe O'Rourke signed Ernie to his first real contract. The Hornets had plenty of outfielders, and Ralph, who was still considered a better prospect, was left behind while Ernie became Philly's hometown hero. He played his first two seasons in Charlotte (1919 and 1920) and thrived under O'Rourke's tutelage. He batted .305 and .346 in those two seasons.

He drew rave reviews for his fielding, especially his quickness in getting to the ball and strong arm, and also his base-running instincts. He led the Hornets in stolen bases in both seasons. Here is an unknown sportswriter's description of one of Ernie's base running exploits in 1919 against pitcher Grady McClung and the Augusta Wolves:

"Padgett opened the sixth with a walk and Holland hoisted a fly ball to left with no advance. Snyder walked, moving

Padgett to second. Padgett danced off second and when McClung threw to get him out, Padgett dug out for third and beat Griffin's tag. Hood then lifted a sacrifice fly to plate Padgett."

"Dug out for third?!" Definitely Pulitzer Prize material!

For Ernie, 1919 was a busy year. He married my grandmother Edith (Edie) and their first child Joe, my namesake, was born in 1920. Edie kept a wonderful scrapbook with which she surprised Ernie for Christmas in 1956. She later gave it to me and it is one of my most-prized possessions. Much of the information in this book has been gleaned from the scrapbook, since Edie saved everything, including newspaper articles, photos, letters, schedules, train tickets, programs, contracts, and more. The first part of this book practically wrote itself. Thanks, Edie.

I have spent countless hours reading the articles and letters and looking at old photos. Some of the newspaper articles are priceless. The sportswriters of the day (picture Max Mercy in *The Natural*) used strange and yet wonderful language that would be considered anachronistic today but clearly depicted their love for the game, and probably seemed colorful at the time. Many were also accomplished cartoonists, creating delightful descriptive scenarios with pen and ink. Unfortunately, many of the newspapers and writers who wrote the articles are unknown. Edie only saved the clippings, not necessarily the bylines.

An early article by an unknown writer in a Charlotte paper is quoted here with the headline:

PADGETT IS THE STUFF

"The addition of Ernie Padgett is probably the best move yet made in strengthening the team. Ernie looks so darn good it is hard to start writing about him without using too many superlatives. Sufficient to say that he has added enough strength to the team to make everyone consider it a real pennant threat."

Yes, I know...that last sentence is grammatically incorrect, and I don't think it was written by Grantland Rice or Ring Lardner, but it's a nice tribute and fun to read. Some sports section headlines of those days include "BEES POUND PILL," and "MCCLUNG IS BESTED," "LEFTY BRUNER GETS GATE," and one of my favorites, "INSECTS STING 6 to 2." Along with the Hornets, the Sally League included teams with nicknames like the Greenville Spinners, Augusta Wolves, Spartanburg Spartans, and the Columbia Comers. I'm not sure what a 'Comer' is. I guess you had to be there.

In 1921 Ernie was traded to the Winston-Salem Twins where he was briefly united with his brother, who had been left behind in Philly. Ralph had the proverbial 'cup of coffee' in professional baseball for only one season before returning to the semi-pro circuit in Philadelphia where he could be closer to his growing family. Ernie continued to thrive in Winston-Salem, where one writer called him "the crack shortstop of the Piedmont League." Once again, he batted over .300 and was among the league leaders in stolen bases and fielding percentage.

In 1922 he was traded back to Charlotte and had another outstanding year, leading all Sally League shortstops on defense while batting .333 for the season. At the end of the season, he was sold to the Memphis Chickasaws ('Chicks') of the Southern Association of Baseball Clubs, an affiliate of the Boston Braves, where he played the entire 1923 season.

Evidently my grandmother Edie didn't care for Memphis, and knowing her as I did (later, of course), I'm sure she badgered Ernie into writing a letter almost two months into the 1923 season to Christy Mathewson, the legendary Hall of Famer who was then part owner and president of the Boston Braves. In the letter, Ernie wrote that the Memphis summer climate "did not agree" with his wife and young son.

As I think about it now, it was probably more than the climate that made Edie uncomfortable. She was a young, northern city girl used to a certain lifestyle and customs, and life in the South in the 1920s in a strange city was probably a major culture shock. I'm sure she couldn't understand the southern accents and they certainly couldn't understand hers. Anyone who has ever heard a Philly accent will know what I mean. I don't have a copy of the letter from Ernie to Christy Mathewson, and while I would love to see it, I'm not surprised that Edie didn't add it to the scrapbook.

BOSTON NATIONAL LEAGUE BASE BALL COMPANY
BRAVES FIELD, BOSTONS

May 26th, 1923.

Mr. Ernest K. Padgett,
C/o Memphis Base Ball Club,
Memphis, Tenn.

Dear Ernest:

I am in receipt of your letter of May 23d saying that the climate at Memphis doesnot agree with you and is very unsatisfactory for your wife and son.

I am taking up this matter with Johnnie Dobbs and enclose herewith a copy of my letter to him. He will doubtless give the matter immediate consideration.

Under the rules the Memphis Club has first claim on your services, consequently we are not at liberty to place you elsewhere, except with the consent of the Memphis Club. If they decide that you cannot give your best services there because of climatic conditions we will make an immediate effort to place you elsewhere.

Very sincerely yours,

Christy Mathewson
President.

(Enclosure).

Included here is the return letter from Mathewson basically commiserating or simply being diplomatic, but patiently explaining to the Padgett duo that the decision to move (or not move) Ernie to another team rested entirely with the Memphis management. Obviously, the Memphis club decided to keep Ernie in Memphis, and Edie's complaints notwithstanding, he went on to have an outstanding season.

Here's another colorful description of Ernie's play at second base by an unknown Memphis writer: "Ernie Padgett, the Chickasaw middle man, is the leading keystoner in the Southern Association from every viewpoint. Padgett had a fine year with the stick this year being in the select .300 circle among the hitters and having been right up in front for some time. Padgett covers a world of ground around the second station and rarely ever lets a drive get through him. He is fast, can go to either side and get 'em. He has also stolen around 20 sacks this season."

As I mentioned earlier, Edie kept a meticulous scrapbook. My absolute favorite photo in the book is of Ernie, surrounded by his Memphis teammates, *picking the pocket* of Commissioner Judge Kennesaw "Mountain" Landis before a game. Landis, known for a non-existent sense of humor, was also known to have his pockets filled with peanuts before arriving at the ballpark because he was too cheap to buy them from a vendor. The expressions on the faces of Ernie's teammates are priceless.

Ernie batted .317 in 122 games and impressed Christy Mathewson and the Boston Braves management enough to bring him to the big club in mid-September of 1923. He appeared in only four games, as noted earlier. However, on October 6th, he had his moment of glory; a play that took less than ten seconds, and is still talked about in baseball circles almost 100 years later.

The Majors

While Ernie certainly ended the 1923 season on a high note, the 1924 season began on a low one. His salary with Memphis for the 1923 season was $350 per month, and as noted in the contracts, players had to not only purchase their own cleats, but also had to pay a $30 deposit for two uniforms, to be refunded when the uniforms were turned in at the end of the season. The major league contracts included the same clauses. I wonder how often those heavy wool/flannel uniforms were laundered.

Once again, I'm sure Edie had a lot to do with it, but Ernie refused to sign the initial 1924 contract tendered by Christy Mathewson and the Braves management.

I can only imagine the ensuing conversation between Edie and Ernie. Nevertheless, Ernie held out, and in a letter dated January 31, 1924 (I would bet my favorite bat that Edie dictated it), Ernie asked for a raise. I have never found a copy of that letter either, but Mathewson referenced the date in his return letter. It's easy to detect a note of impatience on the part of Christy Mathewson. He was accustomed to dealing with ballplayers and their respective personalities, but I can't help but wonder if by this time he was thinking he had a pair of problem children on his hands in Ernie and Edie; the young player and his 'wife, agent and chief negotiator.' In any case, Ernie signed for the additional $150, returned the contract and got ready for spring training and life in "The Show."

BOSTON NATIONAL LEAGUE BASE BALL COMPANY
BRAVES FIELD, BOSTON

January 26th, 1924

Mr. Ernest K. Padgett,

Philadelphia, Pa.

My dear Mr. Padgett:

I am enclosing contract in duplicate calling for twenty-five hundred fifty ($2550) dollars for your services for the season of 1924. Kindly sign and return one copy to this office retaining the other for your own use.

This is a very sizeable increase over what you received last year and I hope that you will demonstrate that you are worth it.

Very truly yours,

C. Mathewson

PRESIDENT.

20

BOSTON NATIONAL LEAGUE BASE BALL COMPANY
BRAVES FIELD, BOSTON

February 15th, 1934

Mr. Ernest K. Padgett,
Philadelphia, Pa.

My dear Padgett:

I have your letter of January 31st and am sorry to hear that you are dissatisfied with the salary. You must admit that the increase mentioned in the contract sent you is very sizeable. However, we do not wish to have any man under contract who feels that he is not receiving enough to live on. Although you say you take the best of care of your money I am sure that with a little better management you could save instead of running behind out of the salary we have offered you. I hope you will find that this is the case and to get you started in the right direction I am enclosing a contract which calls for a still further increase to $2700. Please sign and return this to this office at once.

Very truly yours,

PRESIDENT.

Another Quirk of Fate

During the winter of 1923-24, there was much speculation as well as a good bit of optimism on the part of the Boston sportswriters concerning the future of the Braves. Manager Fred Mitchell, hired away from the Chicago Cubs after leading the Cubs to the National League Pennant in 1918, had a dismal record of 107 and 200 for the 1922-23 seasons with the Braves. He was fired and replaced by 1971 Hall of Fame inductee Dave Bancroft, who became player/manager. He was an outstanding shortstop who would help to solidify the infield. Several young prospects were signed and invited to spring training with the big club, including Ernie Padgett. Things were looking up.

And then a quirk of fate in the form of a tragedy occurred. Tony Boeckel, the Braves' starting third baseman from 1919 through 1923, was killed in an automobile accident in San Diego. The fateful crash happened on February 15 when Boeckel's car collided on a dark highway, meeting head-on with a truck that was without headlights. Uninjured in the collision, Boeckel climbed out of his car to survey the damage, was struck by an oncoming car and died in the hospital the next day. Ironically, Tony had played alongside Ernie in the first game of the 1923 season-ending doubleheader against the Phillies, initiating two double plays. Boeckel collected his final major league hit in that, his final game. A further irony was that Ernie became the Braves regular third baseman in

1924. During that season, the Braves wore black arm bands on their jerseys in honor of Tony Boeckel.

Padgett, Local Product, Among Recruits Making Good This Year

Philadelphia Boy, Who Filled Ill-Fated Tony Boeckel's
Shoes For Braves, Starring On Third—Big
Increase in Young Regulars is Noticeable

Spring training in 1924 was an exciting time for several of the youngsters who were striving to not only become part of the team but to become starters. After several forgettable seasons, there were only a few positions that were not up for grabs. Many of the Boston writers who had witnessed Ernie's unassisted triple play the previous October penned glowing reports of the progress the new prospects were making, including the following article by veteran sportswriter Burton Whitman of the *Boston Herald*.

Whitman could have been the president of the Ernie Padgett Fan Club during spring training. In the following article that appeared in the *Herald*, he wrote, "It is almost a lead pipe cinch that red-headed Ernie Padgett will be a regular for the Braves outfit this season." He went on to rave about Ernie's speed and aggressive base-running.

Padgett and Lucas Look Like Sure-Enough Prospects For Regular Berths on Braves

Red Headed Ernie Is the First Man on the Field Each Day and Has to Be Chased off at Night

By BURTON WHITMAN

ST. PETERSBURG, Fla., March 12—It is almost a lead pipe cinch that red-headed Ernie Padgett and Bricktop Fred Lucas will be regular members of the Braves outfit this season. Manager Dave Bancroft thinks well of both.

Padgett has had just the extra seasoning he needed a year ago this time. He makes a strong appeal with the expert manner in which he handles the ball, and he is alert, aggressive and faster than most of the older infielders with the Tribe.

It would not be a mite surprising if Ernie managed to start the season as a regular. He already has shown enough to warrant his getting a good chance to show his steady gait in the exhibition games against various big league teams here in Florida.

The next day, March 13th, Burton wrote another glowing article, quoting newly hired Braves manager Dave Bancroft, who spoke of Ernie in superlatives, again in the baseball jargon of the 1920s.

Bancroft tells Whitman, "I never saw anyone who could go over and in back of second base and get them any better than this kid Padgett." Whitman writes that this is "as positive a statement of praise as Banny has made in training camp this year."

25

Braves Manager Says Memphis Kid Is a Bear in Picking off Drives Back of Second Base

Youngster Has Improved Tremendously Since Last Year and Displays Real Power With Bludgeon

By BURTON WHITMAN

ST. PETERSBURG, Fla., March 13—"I never saw anyone who could go over and in back of second base and get them any better than this kid Padgett," declared Manager Davey Bancroft of the Boston Braves this morning.

"I once played with a minor leaguer who was as good as Padgett in going back of second base from the regular second position for grounders, but that minor leaguer did not look so much like a batter as does Padgett, and did not have the polish and the smoothness that marks Padgett's work."

Padgett Has Gained Much Confidence

This, fans, is as positive a statement of praise as Banny has made in training camp this year. He is justified in his sweet words for red-headed Ernie Padgett, however. This boy seems to have improved several hundred per cent. over what he showed here a year ago. His sojourn in the minor league, with Memphis, to be exact, gave him experience and added confidence.

"It is not so much the ball over and back of second which Padgett gets," continued Banny, "as it is that he gets them in position to throw. He does not waste any time. He has the idea that is the secret of all good infielding—which is to get that ball over to first or any other base for which you are making the play, without the loss of a fraction of a second."

Hits All Kinds of Pitching and Throws Well

Padgett is quiet, but he has been hitting the ball to left and to right field against various pitching here. He also is given credit for having one of those light throws, which means that the man on the receiving end has an easy time making the catch and that it does not sting his hands as do some good throwers.

SPRING TRAINING 1924

"Hot Potato"

Ernie the Fisherman

Bathing Beauties, Edie and Ernie

Two weeks later, Burton's headline read: "PADGETT'S GREAT WORK COMPLICATES PROBLEM OF SELECTING INFIELD" and the sub-heading: "Fielding and Hitting of Braves Third Base Rookie Phenom Brands Him as One to be Reckoned With."

Ernie began the 1924 season as the starting third baseman for the Braves. He played in 138 games, which was the second highest on the team. Despite having Bancroft, a new and optimistic manager and a couple of promising young players along with several proven veterans like Johnny Cooney, "Stuffy" McInnis, Hall of Fame pitcher Richard "Rube" Marquard, and one of baseball's all-time characters, Casey Stengel, the Braves and their fans endured another last place finish. Their record was 53 and 100, only one less loss than in 1923, probably due to a rain-out that was not made up.

Braves infield 1924, L to R: Stuffy McInnis, Ernie Padgett, Bob Smith, Hunter Lane.

Ernie batted .255 for the season, finishing third in fielding percentage among National League third basemen. As painful as it was for me to realize, he was not living up to the hype. However, he did have some memorable moments in 1924, one of which was the birth of my mother Norma on July 22nd. As a father of a colicky baby girl myself, I understand how sleepless nights can affect anyone's daily routine, especially an athlete. With a four-year old already on board and a new baby in the house without amenities like air-conditioning, a microwave to heat a two A.M. bottle, and no such thing as mobile diaper service (or even disposable diapers), Ernie's batting average may have suffered a bit.

Ernie's one other highlight in 1924 came during a series with the Phillies in his home city. Before the game on June

23rd, Ernie was honored by the Philadelphia fans and proud local sports officials who presented him with several gifts including a diamond ring. I would like to think that Ernie had a great game that day, but Edie didn't include the box score in the scrapbook. I guess he didn't.

Ernie Becomes a Utility Player

The 1925 season began almost the same way as the previous season for the Padgett family. On February 3rd, Christy Mathewson sent Ernie a contract calling for $3,000 for the season, an increase of $250 from 1924. Mathewson's cover letter was cordial but business-like. There was no specific mention of the raise or any comments about it. At the end of the letter he wrote, "Trusting you have had a pleasant winter... ."

Now a father of two, Ernie (I'm sure with Edie's prodding) again asked for more money. This time I would bet my favorite glove that Edie dictated the letter. Once again, a copy was never found. Mathewson did not waver. He sent Ernie a terse, no-nonsense letter dated February 13, 1925, basically telling Ernie that the discussion is over. Take it or leave it.

This time the problem children, Ernie and Edie, probably realized that the glitter of Ernie's unassisted triple play had tarnished a bit. They recognized that they should probably quit while they were ahead. Perhaps, they did not want to cause Christy Mathewson any more heartburn than they already had. Ernie signed the contract.

Evidently, spring training 1925 was not as exciting for the Boston or Philadelphia sportswriters because there are no clippings in Edie's scrapbook. It seems like they used up the superlatives prior to the 1924 season, and the last place finish put a damper on any real optimism. With few additions of note to the roster, the 1925 season was more of the same, with a 7th place finish and a record of 66 and 86.

Ernie did manage to bat .305, only playing in 86 games, mostly at second base and shortstop, having played 113 games at third base the previous season. He had lost his starting job. Future Hall of Fame pitcher Rube Marquard finished the '25 season with a disappointing 2 and 8 record. Casey Stengel batted a meager .077 in only 12 games and was released on May 25th, ending his major league career as a player. I can't help but wonder if his cantankerous and *profane* disposition had something to do with Mathewson's decision to let him go. One of Christy's many nicknames was 'The Christian Gentleman,' and Stengel did not especially project Christian values.

The worst news, however, from the '25 season came on October 7th, with the death of Christy Mathewson at the young age of 45. "Matty" had served on the front lines in France during The Great War, was exposed to mustard gas and later developed tuberculosis which ultimately killed him. He died at his home in Saranac Lake, New York, and was buried in Lewisburg, Pennsylvania, adjacent to the campus of his beloved alma mater, Bucknell University. Arguably, he was the greatest pitcher of all-time, loved, and respected by those who knew him or knew of him, it was the final blow to the reeling Braves and time for another overhaul.

The new president of the Braves was Mathewson's former partner Emil Fuchs, an attorney and former Deputy Attorney General of New York, notorious not only for poor monetary decisions and sleazy deals, but also his poor management of the Braves. While Mathewson was president from 1922 through 1925, Fuchs was listed as vice president on the Braves letterhead until 1926 when he became president. The Braves' fortunes, while dismal at the time, under Fuchs, went further downhill.

A letter dated February 1, 1926, to Ernie from Braves secretary Edwin Riley included a contract calling for an increased salary in the amount of $4,300, a nice increase from $3,000 the previous year. The Padgetts apparently were happy, so Ernie signed and returned the contract. In Riley's letter, beneath the letterhead, "SPRING TRIP REPORTING NOTICE," he noted the reporting date of February 26, and included a check for $54.52 for railroad and pullman tickets. Riley also added a reminder, "Don't forget your baseball shoes, gloves, sweater and whatever other paraphernalia you'll need at Training Camp."

Once again, there are no clippings or articles by the Boston sportswriters in the scrapbook about Ernie or about spring training in general. Edie and the kids did not accompany Ernie to Florida, and probably (more likely) the writing was on the wall because Ernie's contract was sold to the Cleveland Indians of the American League and he was given his "Notice of Transfer" in the form of a postcard on April 6, 1926. He went from St. Petersburg to Lakeland in one day, essentially from Boston to Cleveland to start the season. I could not find out how much Cleveland paid for Ernie's contract. Since there was no trade, penny-pinching Emil Fuchs banked whatever the Indians paid, and saved $4,300, less the $54.52 that Riley had sent for travel expenses.

NOTICE TO PLAYER

No. 189

NOTICE TO PLAYER OF RELEASE OR TRANSFER
NATIONAL LEAGUE

April 6th, , 192 6

To Mr. Ernest K. Padgett

You are hereby notified as follows:

1. ~~That your are unconditionally released.~~
2. That your contract has been assigned to the _____ Cleveland
   Club of _____ American _____ League.　　(a) Without right of recall.
   　　　　　　　　　　　　　　　　　　　~~(b) With right of recall.~~

(Cross out parts not applicable. In case of optional agreement, specify all conditions affecting player.)

Boston National League Base Ball Co.
　　　　　　　　　　　　　　　　Corporate Name of Club.

Ernie Quinn
　　　　　　　　　　　　　　　　President.

Copy must be delivered to player; also forwarded to President of League of which Club is a member, and to the Commissioner.

Ernie must have decided to keep his 1924 wool/flannel Braves jersey. I've always assumed he simply decided to give up his deposit, because I ended up with the jersey along with one of his gloves, his Cleveland cap, and a couple of Ernie "Red" Padgett 35 oz. Louisville Slugger bats. I'll never know how a little guy could swing such heavy lumber. Maybe that's why he was described as a "slap hitter," with only one home run to his credit.

Ernie's Cleveland contract, dated April 13, 1926, called for another nice increase to $5,000 for the season. The Indians planned to use Ernie as a temporary replacement for their regular second baseman, Johnny Hodapp, who was recovering from a serious ankle injury. Ernie played in only 36 games, batting a career low of .210 while playing respectably at second base, but not well enough to dislodge

Hodapp from his position when he returned from his injury. Cleveland had a good season in 1926 under the direction of Hall of Fame player/manager Tris Speaker, nicknamed 'the Gray Ghost' for his impeccable play in center field.

The Indians finished second to the Yankees, three games back, with a record of 88 and 66. Meanwhile, in the other league, the hapless Braves finished 50 and 103, again in 7th place.

There were a few bright spots for Ernie in 1926 in Cleveland, including having teammates like future Hall of Famers Joe Sewell and Tris Speaker, and 1926 MVP first baseman George Burns, who, as I mentioned above, also made an unassisted triple play in 1923. I still have a baseball autographed by most of the 1926 Indians, including Speaker.

The second bright spot was a full-page ad and an endorsement by Ernie and three of his teammates for Studebaker Automobiles. Ernie was given a 1927 Studebaker "Standard Six Custom Sedan." In the magazine photo, Ernie is sitting on the front bumper. I know Edie was proud of that. The third bright spot for the Padgetts in 1926 came in the form of a monetary windfall. Having finished in second place in the American League (There were no divisions or Wild Card teams in those days.), the Cleveland players each received a check on October 11 from the Commissioner's Office for $621.25. I am sure that Ernie, Edie, Joe, and Norma had a nice Christmas and travelled in style back to their home in Philly in the new Studebaker.

In one of the few games in which he did play, late in the 1926 season, Ernie suffered a serious leg injury on an attempted steal, which nagged him through the winter and into the start of 1927 spring training. Obviously, there was no such thing as sports medicine in those days and whatever the injury was, it bothered him for the rest of his life. As a kid I remember him limping, and sometimes I watched him rub liniment on his leg, but he told me in his modest way that it was simply a matter of old age creeping up. For the last years of his life, he used a cane.

I did find one reference to Ernie's injury in the January 31 letter from Ernest S. Barnard, Cleveland club president and later president of the American League, which accompanied his 1927 contract. The contract called for the same $5,000 salary as in 1926, and in the letter, Barnard basically apologized for not increasing Ernie's salary, based on "uncertainties of what the season has in store for us all." At the end of this same letter Barnard wrote, "Heard you were injured last fall but hope that you have fully recovered and that the injury will not interfere with your work this year."

Ernie signed and returned the contract. A follow-up letter from Barnard on February 14 included a detailed travel itinerary to spring training in Lakeland. This time Edie also decided to stay home in Philadelphia with their two children. Tris Speaker was no longer the Indians' manager, having resigned over a contract dispute and gone to the Washington Senators at the end of the 1926 season. He was replaced by first-time manager Jack McCallister, who had never played a game in the big leagues. His tenure lasted exactly one year, taking the Indians in the wrong direction from a second-place finish in 1926 under Speaker, to a sixth-place finish in 1927 with a 66 and 87 record. Tris Speaker and his steady leadership were sorely missed, and like the Braves, the Indians' fortunes were unraveling.

McCallister was fired at the end of the season and never managed a major league team again. E.S. Barnard resigned as club president to become president of the American League, working for former federal judge and arbiter of the 1919 Black Sox Scandal, Commissioner Kennesaw "Mountain" Landis.

Ernie's injury affected his performance on the field and he was released on July 30 having appeared in only seven games, and batting .286. His major league career was over. He went home to Philly to nurse his injury and perhaps his wounded pride. But like most old ballplayers, including yours truly, the fire still burns inside and the nagging thought keeps coming back: "I *know* I can do this at least *one* more season, pain be damned. I want *one* more season. Then I'll quit. Maybe. But hey, my glove is hardly broken in and I have two new bats." I've been saying this for more than twenty years, along with some of my long-time teammates. We all agree that if we ever start to embarrass ourselves or the team, we'll quit. So far, so good.

In Ernie's case I don't know for sure, and I was always too young to have that kind of discussion with him, but I'm sure he felt like there might somehow be a path back to the major leagues, his leg injury notwithstanding. However, the Padgett family still needed the breadwinner to keep bringing home the paychecks, so while Edie managed their home, Ernie took a job in the fall of 1927 in Philly selling wallpaper paste.

He kept his passion for baseball alive and earned some pocket money by once again playing semi-pro baseball with the Brooklyn Bushwicks during the fall, playing such teams as The House of David Baseball Club, a team of bearded Jewish players. Knowing Edie as I did, I'm sure Ernie didn't get to keep much of that extra money in his pocket. By the time winter came, he was already thinking of playing baseball somewhere in the spring.

After releasing Ernie in July of 1927, the Cleveland Indians sold his contract to the New Orleans Pelicans, an unaffiliated Southern Association 'A' Ball team. In a letter in the fall of 1927 to the New Orleans management, Ernie asked to be placed on the Voluntarily Retired List. Quite possibly his decision had something to do with his leg injury and knowing that he could not live up to the standard of play that he set for himself. I have a hard time believing that he enjoyed selling wallpaper paste.

Clearly disappointed and now owning the contract of a player who was retiring from baseball, A.J. Heinemann, the Pelicans' owner, sent a letter to Ernie on February 20, 1928, basically telling Ernie that if he would spend a season with the Pelicans, he might make his way back to the majors. Heinemann was basically trying to charm Ernie into playing, without mentioning the simple fact that the Pelicans would be losing money if Ernie ultimately decided not to play. The letter appears below.

A. J. HEINEMANN, PRESIDENT   LARRY GILBERT, MANAGER

The New Orleans Baseball and Amusement Co.
==== LIMITED ====

OPERATING

THE NEW ORLEANS BASEBALL CLUB

OFFICE AND GROUNDS
HEINEMANN PARK

THE LARGEST PLAYING GROUNDS IN THE UNITED STATES
8 PENNANT WINNERS OF THE SOUTHERN LEAGUE

PHONES: GALVEZ
9440—9441—9442

NEW ORLEANS, LA.   Feb. 20th, 1928

Mr. Ernest Padget,
Philadelphia, Pa.

Dear Sir,

Received your letter and was surprised at a young man of your age would want to be placed on the voluntarily retired list, a year down here would help you that you would be able to go back in the Majors where you belong, you know what is the trouble, you played in so few games last year that the Major league clubs were scared of you on account of your leg.

As can at You know that you can make more money playing ball than you can at anything else. We are lining up a good ball club, and we always play Texas league series which means extra money for you.

Lets see if we can't get together, You know with men like Benny Karr, Joe Martins, Eichrodt, Danforth. Tucker and others with this class of men you will be on a good club.

With best personal regards from Larry and myself I beg to remain.

Sincerely yours,

[signature] J.H. Heinemann

Benny Karr, George "Ike" Eichrodt, and Dave Danforth had all been teammates of Ernie's in Cleveland the previous season, and had obviously been casualties of the restructuring of the team. This gave Ernie something else to think about, being united with guys that he knew. While he wrestled with his decision and continued to peddle wallpaper paste, a cold Philadelphia winter set in. I have no doubt that he had many sleepless nights wondering if he should try to get back into professional baseball.

It was a big decision: Continue selling wallpaper paste or play baseball? I would love to have been privy to *that* conversation between Ernie and Edie. I wonder if he gave the wallpaper paste company two weeks' notice?

Reverse the Charges

A couple of long-distance phone calls opened the door. I found a wonderful article about those phone calls in Edie's scrapbook by *Philadelphia Inquirer* sportswriter Stan Baumgartner, a former major league pitcher who had a real penchant for dialogue, and obviously an ironic sense of humor. His depiction of events is hilarious. In the article it becomes obvious that some of Edie's hard line bargaining style had rubbed off on Ernie. As a kid, I knew that he was an easy-going, modest man of few words, but when he did speak, people listened. I sure did. I guess he was a man of few words in 1927 as well, as the article shows.

At the time, Ernie was selling wallpaper paste in Philly, and Baumgartner writes that Ernie was "apparently deeply engrossed in his business," having retired from baseball despite the fact that the New Orleans Pelicans now owned his contract. Baumgartner writes that Ernie told the Pelicans to "put his contract in camphor. He was through."

The Pelicans didn't want to take "no" for an answer, and in a telegram to Ernie, Pelicans manager Larry Gilbert asked Ernie to call him and reverse the charges. Ernie did, and when Gilbert asked what it would take to come and play for the Pelicans, Ernie was quick to answer, saying he wanted $500 a month, transportation both ways, and an electric refrigeration plant for his room. (The term air conditioning hadn't been invented yet.) The subsequent exchange is priceless, yet at the end of the negotiation, in the final phone call, Gilbert told

Ernie, "The old man (Heineman) says he will give you the salary and transportation, but he'll be blasted if he will furnish cold air during the summer!" Ernie looked out the window at the snow falling in Philly and told Gilbert, "Gil, I'll be on my way tomorrow night. Have a few warmers ready for me and don't spill them."

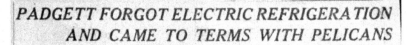

PADGETT FORGOT ELECTRIC REFRIGERATION AND CAME TO TERMS WITH PELICANS

Waft of Cold Air Convinced Ernie He Needed No Cooling Apparatus

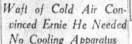

By STAN BAUMGARTNER

ERNIE PADGETT, shortstop par excellence, and last year a member of the Cleveland Indians, is today basking in the sunshine of New Orleans, ready to pounce in the Pelican line-up.

But it took $33.95 worth of long-distance telephone calls from the Southern city to clinch the bargain.

Up to last Friday Padgett was a salesman for a wall paper paste concern. He was apparently deeply engrossed in his business and was playing independent baseball merely to pad his pocketbook. Ernie had notified the New Orleans Club to which he had been sold during the winter to put his 1928 contract in camphor. Padgett was "through." He had retired.

His apparent seriousness baffled the New Orleans Club and also led Nat Strong, manager of the Brooklyn Bushwicks to tender him an independent contract. Padgett signed and for three weeks cavorted about the diamond in Brooklyn.

Friday the 13th, however, brought bad luck to the New York manager. Ernie received a telegram from Larry Gilbert, manager of the New Orleans Club, requesting the local ball tosser to telephone New Orleans and reverse the charges. When the telephone buzzed in the southern city, Gilbert was at the receiver.

"How much salary do you want to play with my ball club?" queried the New Orleans pilot.

"I'll take $—— a month, and transportation both ways. You might also add an electric refrigerator plant for my room during the torrid summer months," replied Ernie.

Padgett Accepts

"YOU'LL take what?" asked the stunned Gilbert. "Padgett if I asked the 'old man' (the New Orleans owner) for that much money he would think I wanted to sign a regiment of shortstops. Say Kid, no foolin, now, did you strike oil or do dollars grow on trees in Philadelphia?"

"Larry, those are my terms," answered Padgett.

"Well good-bye then," concluded Gilbert.

But Saturday morning Padgett was again called to the phone.

"The old man says he will give you the salary and transportation but he'll be blasted if he will furnish cold air during the summer," spoke Gilbert.

Just then Padgett looked out the window, saw the snow flakes dropping down, shivered a bit, thought of the warm breezes of New Orleans and shouted.

"Gil, it can't get too hot for me, I'll be on my way tomorrow night, have a few warmers ready for me and don't spill them."

Goes South

ERNIE PADGETT

*New Orleans Pelicans, 1928; Ernie Padgett, front row,
second from the right.*

Ernie played for the Pelicans in 1928. In 137 games with 501 plate appearances, he batted .322. He had been given a raise in 1928 bringing his salary to $600 a month, but *without* air conditioning. While he was offered a contract by the Pelicans for the 1929 season, he declined the offer. Perhaps the New Orleans heat was finally getting to him. Maybe he missed his family, or his leg injury was getting worse. We'll never know.

In 1930 he decided to give it one last shot and he signed with his old team, the Charlotte Hornets. In half a season in Charlotte he found his old groove at the plate and batted .316. For whatever reason, he left the Hornets in mid-season and went home to Philly. I never found out if he went back to selling wallpaper paste, but he signed with the Reading

Keystones, an industrial league team. After only 94 at-bats, he suffered a broken leg and his baseball career ended for good. I never found out if the broken leg was a new injury or a residual effect of his injury in 1926. That too, we will never know.

Baseball was over for Ernie and it was time to enter the real world of a 9 to 5 job and raising a family. I have known and been friends with several former big-league players. Every one of them told me that one of the biggest adjustments in their lives and the lives of their families came the first time they did not go to spring training. Some were philosophical about it, realizing that they had been well-paid to play a game, a great game for sure, but nevertheless a game. Many had made smart investments and were financially set for life. Some stayed connected to the game as scouts, announcers, and coaches. Some wrote books. There have been a few suicides and quite a few divorces. Many traded on their former celebrity to sell cars, insurance, miracle drugs, beer, spray paint, and even wallpaper paste.

Life After Baseball

Back home for good now in Philly, Ernie settled into domestic life and the business of raising kids. My Uncle Joe and Norma (my mother) were now ten and six, respectively. Ernie also took a job with Gibbs Underwear Company as a salesman. Perhaps his previous experience selling wallpaper paste provided some insight into the new job. Later, he became an executive, and I always remember him as a dapper gentleman in a three-piece suit, pocket watch on a gold chain and an elegant tie. I also remember Edie handing him a beer when he got home.

Ernie at his desk at the Gibbs Underwear Company, Philadelphia

At some point Ernie tried to interest young Joe in playing baseball. He was a gifted athlete and showed potential to become a fine ballplayer. However, as a youngster he faced a lot of pressure from peers and coaches because his dad had been a major leaguer. He was expected to live up to Ernie's legacy and was constantly hearing about "what your dad did." As a result, he walked away from baseball.

Ernie, demonstrating his capacity for empathy, understanding, and patience which I came to love, did not push Joe to play baseball as many parents do today. Instead, Joe gravitated toward soccer and basketball, becoming a standout at Olney High School in both sports. I have a box of old tarnished medals and faded ribbons that he received from grade school on up through high school for not only athletic achievement, but academic prowess as well. College scholarships were on the horizon.

In the meantime, Ernie still paid attention to baseball, and was a regular at Shibe Park, later renamed Connie Mack Stadium, as a guest of Major League Baseball and his friend Connie Mack, the legendary owner and manager of the Philadelphia Athletics of the American League. I still have the lifetime passes which were presented to Ernie and Edie for admission to all major league ball parks. Unfortunately, they are not honored now. Today, a family of four almost needs a second mortgage to attend a game.

Ernie became something of a celebrity in his hometown. Later on, when we attended games together, some people still asked for his autograph. As a little kid, I couldn't understand that. Though he never sought attention, quite often the Philly sportswriters would spot him at a game, usually sitting by himself, and question him about young 'up and coming' prospects. He was always willing to offer his views to reporters, and he occasionally did radio interviews.

In 1930, Raymond Hill, a sportswriter for the *Philadelphia Inquirer* spotted Ernie in the grandstand behind home plate at Shibe Park. In an impromptu interview, Hill asked him what he thought about a young Philadelphia Athletics rookie named Edwin Dibrell "Dib" Williams, an Arkansas native who had recently been brought up to the majors by the Athletics. He played five seasons with the A's including the 1931 World Series (won by the Cardinals in seven games).

Unfortunately, like Ernie, Williams never lived up to all the hype, and his star burned out in only a couple of years. After four mediocre seasons with the A's, he was traded to the Red Sox in 1935 and released at the age of 25. Also, like Ernie, Williams wasn't ready to give up baseball just yet. He continued to play in low minors and independent baseball leagues until 1947 when he finally hung up his cleats.

Ernie, who never said an unkind word about anyone, sang the praises of Dib Williams, making such comments as, "Yep, you can take my word for it that Williams is going to be a great ball player. He has as fine a pair of hands as any infielder you can name." Ernie also goes on to say that Williams simply needs more playing time. Speaking from experience at the end of his own career, Ernie says, "Believe me it's no fun sitting on the bench day after day for week after week and then going in and trying to play an unfamiliar position."

Ernie Padgett Thinks Dib Williams, of A's, Has Makings of Great Star

BY RAYMOND A. HILL

"WATCH that fellow closely. He's a fine ball player already. Some day he's going to be one of the great infielders of the league."

Ernie Padgett was talking about Dib Williams, who has been playing shortstop for the Athletics during Joe Boley's enforced absence.

And when Padgett starts talking about infielders he speaks with the knowledge of an expert. Ernie played some fine base ball for the Boston Braves and Cleveland Indians before he quit organized base ball to devote his time to business. Lately he's turned semi-pro for Farnkford Legion and the Brooklyn Bushwicks, yet still finds time to sneak out to Shibe Park ever so often.

"Yep," Ernie went on, "you can take my word for it that Williams is going to be a great ball player. He has as fine a pair of hands as any infielder you can name. It's a delight to watch him field the ball. He's fast and he can hit.

"Oh, I know what you're going to say—he hasn't been throwing any too accurately. Well, let me tell you something. That kid is a natural second baseman. Has a second baseman's arm. Throws strictly over-hand and not enough side-arm or underhand.

"Nevertheless he'd get them over as well as the next fellow from short if he had more opportunity to play. Believe me, it's no fun sitting on the bench day after day for week after week and then going in and trying to play an unfamiliar position.

"Williams deserves a lot of credit for the fine work he's been doing, all things considered. He's a real ball player."

Anent Throwing

IT is true that Williams uses strictly an over-hand motion in throwing the ball. He has a powerful arm but he always straightens up before he lets one go to first base.

This brings to mind a recent conversation with Pie Traynor, Pittsburgh's great third sacker, who is a past master in the art of getting the ball over to first quickly and accurately.

"I never think much about throwing," Pie explained in answer to a query, "My main object is to get the ball away as quickly as possible. I throw it from almost any position as soon as it's been fielded. Naturally, I have my directional bearings. But otherwise I never bother about getting into position for a throw.

"Most big league infielders have two ways of throwing a ball to first base. If the fielder's arm is strong, he'll throw for the first baseman's waist. If his arm is weak, he'll throw for the head and the ball will carry."

This is interesting in view of what Eddie Gottlieb had to say about Dib Williams' throwing. Gottie was a pretty good ball player before he started managing the champion Sphas basket ball team and went in for all other sports on a big basis.

"Williams' main trouble is in his over-hand throwing," Gottie observed. "There is a natural rise on every ball he throws. Since he has been aiming for Foxx's head, the ball has been shooting upward and sometimes out of reach.

"He could overcome this easily by throwing for Foxx's waist. Then the natural rise of the ball could not possibly carry it out of reach before it arrived at first.

* * *

The Highest Price

BASE BALL fans who believe Babe Ruth represents the biggest investment any major league team ever made have another think coming.

So says Ira Thomas, scout of the A's, and he explained himself at the weekly luncheon at the Poor Richard Club yesterday.

"When Connie Mack was putting together his world championship Athletics," said Ira, "he learned that the New York Giants had offered the Portland Club of the Pacific Coast League, $50,000 for a young catcher named Mickey Cochrane.

"The Athletics' scouts were well posted as to Cochrane's natural ability so Mr. Mack lost no time in dispatching a representative to Portland to buy the controlling interest of that team at a price of $160,000. Another $50,000 then was paid for Cochrane's release—an actual purshase price of $210,000 for the finest catcher in all base ball history."

And, boys and girls, even if Babe Ruth does draw down $80,000 per annum, please remember Colonel Jacob Ruppert paid no more than a paltry $137,000 to lure the Bambino away from the Boston Red Sox.

Tragedy

Athlete Dies

JOSEPH PAGET

Injuries in a basketball game claimed the life yesterday of Joseph Paget, 16-year-old son of Ernest Paget, who played professional baseball with the Boston and Cleveland teams a decade ago.

The boy, a sophomore at Olney High Schol, where he was a member of both the basketball and soccer teams, died in Jefferson Hospital, following a kidney operation.

The injury which created the condition, physicians said, occurred in a fall during an Olney-Southern High game Thursday night. Paget was taken to the hospital Saturday after complaining of pains.

Paget was a member of the Hy Wy fraternity, and had played soccer and baseball for the Lighthouse. In addition to his parents he is survived by a sister, Norma. He lived at 4152 Maywood st., Frankford. Funeral services will be held at an undertaking establishment at 11th st and Lehigh ave., Wednesday, at 2:30 P. M., with interment in Northwood

Young Joe Padgett, now 16, was making a name for himself on high school basketball courts. Tall and lanky, unlike Ernie and Edie, college recruiters were watching him closely. On February 22, during a game against a rival school, Joe was involved in a hard collision under the basket. After a brief time on the bench, he checked back into the game. Later that night he complained of pain in his lower back and abdomen. Ernie took him to a hospital, where he was diagnosed with a ruptured kidney. He passed away just a couple hours later. I'm sure that he would have survived that injury in today's world. As a father who knows the terrible pain of losing a child, I know what a deep gaping hole it leaves in your heart. Your life is never the same. I know that was the situation for the Padgetts in 1937. Other than an outpouring of grief and support from friends and some letters of condolence in Edie's scrapbook, I can only speculate on how their lives changed. Mine certainly did when I lost my daughter.

Some things I do know. For my mother, now thirteen, her big brother, her *hero* was gone. She used to tell us stories about Joe. Aside from being a great athlete, he was kind, compassionate and quiet like his dad, but also tough like his mother. He also had a wonderful sense of humor like Ernie.

I know that my mother paid a steep price for Joe's absence, as children surviving a deceased sibling sometimes do. I would prefer to think that it was unintentional, but Edie made life hard for my mother, as parents of lost children also sometimes do. Joe had been the light of Edie's life and that light had been extinguished. My mother told us later that Edie thought the sun rose and set because of Joe. I never met him, of course, but as a kid I actually missed him and loved to hear stories about him because I knew he would have been a wonderful uncle.

My mother also told us that Ernie became something of an introvert, pouring his energy into his work, becoming a foreman at Gibbs Underwear until he retired in the early 1950s. He didn't follow baseball like he once did. He played golf with friends and he drank a lot of beer. He didn't talk much. My mother said it was as if he didn't know how to talk to her anymore, and that broke her heart.

Most evenings, he retreated to his basement workshop where he liked to tinker and repair things that didn't need repairing, and he liked to build things out of wood. He had an old over-stuffed chair in a corner of the basement, and sometimes my mother would sit at the top of the stairs and listen to him sobbing. The frequent twinkle in his eyes that I saw and hoped I had re-kindled, had disappeared in those sad days. I understand that too. A light had gone out for Ernie also. I like to think I helped to bring it back. I spent a lot of time with him in that basement in the 1950s and cherished every second, maybe building a bird house, or simply listening to his explanations of how certain tools worked. I still use his carving chisels and I keep them well-sharpened, as he did.

Edie became an inconsolable, unhappy woman and drinking became her therapy. Her best friend was a quart bottle of Cutty Sark Scotch. While Ernie was in the basement, Edie drank. As much as I hate to write this, she could be a nasty drunk, lashing out at whomever happened to be nearby. My mother could never please her. Even as a kid I remember Edie criticizing my mother for little things and I couldn't understand why. Today I do, having lost two wonderful spouses to terrible illnesses.

I loved Edie. She was my grandmother and she was my buddy. She was always kind to me, and we had a lot of fun together, mostly when she was sober. When she wanted a drink, she told me it was simply time to "take her medicine." Once in a while she let me taste whatever she was drinking. She would say, "Don't tell your mother." We shared secrets and had adventures, scheming together to make Ernie laugh or to piss him off 'in a good way' sometimes. I always had mixed feelings about that. I would have never done anything on purpose to upset Pop Pop Ernie, and I would have done anything to make him smile. I'm sure there were very few smiles in the Padgett house during that sad time.

Edie never stopped missing Joe, and a lot of what I knew about him came from her. Ernie rarely spoke about him to me. Edie (Nana to her grandchildren) was probably the first person who explained to me about the hole in the heart. Somewhere along the way I realized that I was a kind of surrogate for both of them and they frequently vied for my attention. Like most kids, I learned to work the system. I also knew that deep down there lurked in Edie a mean streak. Sometimes I saw it, mostly when she was sticking up for us kids. God have mercy on anyone who wronged her four grandkids; my two brothers, my sister Janine and me. She was a large woman, out-weighing Ernie after a while by quite a bit, and her presence alone was often enough to intimidate.

The Padgetts had a Boston Bulldog named Toby. I loved that dog. They let him sleep with me when I spent nights in Philly. He snorted, had terrible breath and serious gas problems, but he was my pal. Sometimes I'd wake up and find him under the covers with me. Edie used to cook chicken livers for him in the morning. I'm sure that had a lot to do with his bad breath and flatulence. It was a major source of amusement when he would let out a long noxious gas fart, often in his sleep. He would wake up and look at everyone as if to say, "I didn't do that. Which one of you did it?"

Then with a great show of dignity, he would leave the room. Edie loved him; maybe that explains Toby's stinky chicken liver breakfasts.

Norma, Toby, and two of Toby's pups

The greatest thing that Edie ever did in her life, other than marrying Ernie, occurred in 1942. World War II was raging; people were making sacrifices and coming together. Young men were enlisting in the Army, Navy, or Marines, eager to fight for the country. Women who had never worked before were taking jobs in factories to support the war effort. Everyone did his or her part for the common good. With Ernie's blessing, Edie did something pretty remarkable.

Knowing that Joe would have been among the first to enlist, Edie decided that she would take his place. At age 43 she enlisted in the Women's Auxiliary Army Corps (WAAC) as a private, and reported for duty in Des Moines, Iowa on October 10, 1942, where she became one of the oldest recruits.

In the scrapbook there is a wonderful article by an unknown *Philadelphia Inquirer* writer, along with a great photo of Edie teaching Ernie to cook before heading off to basic training in Iowa. Ernie, ever the joker, quips that his triple play in 1923 was easier than making a soufflé, and he will not be baking pies, and will continue getting them from the Automat. Evidently, Edie's attempts at teaching Ernie to cook were a dismal failure.

I remember my mother joking with Ernie about what a terrible cook he was, so she took over the cooking duties while Edie was away. Later on, in the summer I would spend the night with Edie and Ernie so we could get up early and go crabbing. Ernie usually burned the eggs and potatoes. The kitchen filled with smoke and Edie would come out of the bedroom in her nightgown asking if we were trying to set the house on fire. Ernie told her that he wasn't the one doing the cooking, blaming me!

He said he was "just reading the paper while Joey was cooking," while waving the paper around, trying to get the smoke out of the kitchen. Then he winked at me. We had our breakfast that day and many others at a greasy spoon luncheonette called 'The Bazaar' before some of our many adventures.

Other than a few letters from his old teammates and an occasional newspaper reference to triple plays, there is little in the scrapbook about the years between 1942 and 1946, the year I was born. Norma and my father married in 1944 when they were both in the Navy.

Self-Defense: From Shortstop to Stove

Back in 1923 Shortstop Ernie Padgett made baseball history with an unassisted triple play. In 1942 he's learning how to cook. Reason: His wife, Edith, has joined the WAACS, doesn't want him to go hungry while she's away. She has 10 days to teach him all.

'Triple-Play' Padgett Cooks As Wife 'Replaces' Son in Army

Remember Ernie Padgett, the chap who made a triple play unassisted, and got his name into the record books?

He was a shortstop then, but he's staying close to the home plate these days. Learning to cook!

It's a question of self-defense, because his wife, Edith, has signed up as a private with the WAACS, and leaves for Des Moines October 10.

Balks at Pies.

"I'm teaching him," Mrs. Padgett said yesterday, "and he's doing nicely. I think I'll have him on roasts by the time I leave."

"I draw the line at pie, though," said Ernie. "Rather get it at the automat."

The Padgetts live at 4225 M st., where, in a shiny, modern kitchen, "Triple-Play" Ernie takes a daily cooking lesson. Then he's off to the underwear manufacturing company where he's a foreman.

Taking Son's Place.

He and his wife laugh a lot over his mistakes, but the reason for her joining the WAACS is one that deals with sorrow.

Five years ago their only son, Joseph, was fatally injured while playing basketball with Olney High.

"I feel," said Mrs. Padgett, "that I am taking my son's place. If he had lived he would have been 21 now and in the Army."

Isn't Shy About Age.

She has been, still is, working at the Interceptor Command. She also is a member of the bugle corps of the Hunting Park Post, American Legion. She has a daughter, Norma, 18.

"Do you mind my asking your age?" said the reporter.

"Not at all," said Mrs. Padgett. "I'm 43, and they told me I was in perfect physical condition for my age."

Played With Braves.

Her husband is the same age. It was in 1923 that he made his famous play while with the Boston Braves.

The Braves were playing the Phillies. Phillies were on first and second. The batter lined a drive to Ernie at short. Ernie grabbed it, ran over and tagged second, then tagged the runner coming down from first.

"Much easier," Ernie said, "than making a souffle."

57

After my mother passed away in 2013, my sister and my two brothers and I argued about who would get her portrait in her WAVES uniform. I should say who *had* to take it. As an artist, I certainly had the least amount of available wall space (at least that was my excuse). Janine didn't want it, so I think one of my brothers, Danny or David, has it in a closet somewhere. Over the years, I sort of expected that Danny or David (knowing the Seme brothers' collective sense of humor) would send it to me as a Christmas present, at which time it would take up residence in one of my closets. Sorry, Mom.

Two Sailors, Danny and Norma 1944

Down the Shore

I assume that Edie served honorably as a WAAC. I used to wonder how she survived recruit training without her best pal Cutty. I do remember that she liked to spend time at the bar in the American Legion Hall when I was a kid, I suppose swapping lies and war stories. I used to go there with her sometimes. She also liked Cucci's Bar, which was on the waterfront. While she drank with her pals, I often hung out on the dock behind the bar with the fishermen. Sometimes I stayed inside and played shuffleboard.

After the war ended, my mother and father lived for a brief time with my father's Italian family in a third-floor walk-up apartment in Newark; "Nurk," as the locals would say. That apartment would be called a tenement today.

My father's parents, Nellie and John, came from Italy around 1900 and of course, through Ellis Island. When they left Italy, their surname was "Senna." Most likely a bored and overworked clerk filled out their paperwork and like so many immigrants whose names had been arbitrarily changed, their name became "Seme." They couldn't read English and they barely spoke it, so they didn't dispute the name change. They had made it to America.

Grandpa John passed away when I was maybe two or three and I only remember him through stories and a few photos. Nellie, on the other hand, I remember well. By the time I knew her, she was about four feet tall and probably that wide in the middle. She had an impressive mustache and huge, hairy

forearms, probably from rolling dough for her wonderful pasta. What I remember most is that she smelled like garlic and loved to hug me and smother me between her ample breasts. She was a great cook, and I still use her recipes. She also preserved tomatoes and other vegetables from her backyard garden. She made her own vinegar, filling empty Cutty Sark bottles, then lining them up on shelves in her pantry. I remember that apartment, not so much from when we lived there, but from childhood visits.

When I was a toddler, my parents bought a small house in Ocean County "down the shore," as they say in New Jersey. Ernie had been making good money at Gibbs Underwear, so he and Edie had already bought a cottage down the street from ours, not far from the Metedeconk River and Barnegat Bay, and about a ten-minute drive to the ocean.

It was a wonderful place to grow up. There were crabs and fish in the river and bay, clear fresh water in the creeks, wild blueberries everywhere, plenty of woods, wildlife, and cedar swamps for forts and tree houses. There were also lots of farms, famous for Jersey tomatoes. We had a small community beach on the river where I almost drowned my brother Danny. It was an accident, of course, but he never lets me forget it.

This is one of those family stories, so I can't say I actually remember it. I was maybe six months old at the time, but Edie visited us once at Nellie and John's (and Norma and Danny's) crowded apartment in Newark. Evidently, Edie noticed the bottles of Cutty Sark lined up in the pantry while Nellie was showing her around. So goes the story that Edie awoke in the middle of the night with a terrible thirst and in need of some 'medicine.' She tip-toed to the pantry, took a long slug from a Cutty bottle and nearly choked on Nellie's vinegar, waking up everyone but me. I heard later that was her first and only visit to Newark.

After we moved "down the shore," Danny, my father, formed a small marine construction company with a partner named Randall Gant. People were buying up the abundant waterfront property and needed bulkheads and docks, so *Gant and Seme* stayed busy year-round.

Big Dan's truck 1953

Randall and their two long-time employees, 'the crew,' Harry Steel and Jimmy Jackson, were tough, hard-working and equally hard-drinking men, described back then in the New Jersey vernacular as "Pineys," a reference to the folks who lived in the woods in the Pine Barrens of southern Jersey. Here in the South, they would be affectionately called "Rednecks." Jimmy had almost no teeth; Harry was missing an eye, lost during a dispute in a local bar.

There was no such thing as political correctness in those days, so the crew referred to Danny as the "WOP" in charge, and his tender nickname for them, as I remember, was "shit kickers." It was all good, and they would have done anything for each other. They were strong men doing extremely hard work.

The lumber in those days was treated with creosote, black, noxious and smelly, and would burn the skin. All four men had the scars to prove it. They all worked with their shirts off in the summer and their muscled upper bodies were almost as dark as the lumber. My father hired college boys as summer help, but after suffering from severe sunburn and creosote burns, they rarely lasted more than a week.

Randall was also a Piney, basically as uneducated as Harry and Jimmy, but he was honest and hard-working, and the business thrived. My father and Randall worked in the water alongside Harry and Jimmy, both during the heat of the summer and in the frigid New Jersey winters of the 1950s.

If you didn't know, you would never be able to figure out which men were the bosses and which men made up the crew. There was no such thing as Gore-Tex or insulated neoprene in those days. Waders and hip boots were made of rubber, and in the winter my father came home from work most afternoons chilled to the bone, usually smelling like beer and creosote, which always seemed normal to me. Big and strong, he would often wrestle with my brother Danny and me in the living room until together we pinned him (he let us) and he usually fell asleep on the floor until dinner time. My father was also the first person I remember who wore his red baseball cap backward. He was probably the toughest man I ever knew.

Ernie (Pop Pop to me) liked to visit the job sites, usually against Edie's wishes. I know they argued about it because she thought my profane Italian father was a bad influence on Ernie. He usually used the excuse "I'm just taking Joey to see his Dad," so he could hang out with the crew. More than that, he liked to stop at the Red Lion Tavern or Cucci's Bar with them at the end of the day. His sound reasoning occurred to me later, but we always seemed to visit the job sites late in the day, usually just before quitting time.

I would go swimming or catch big blue crabs along the shore with my dip net, or I listened to the crew banter back and forth while they were working. They would tease me about potential girlfriends while Ernie retrieved a cold beer from the crew's cooler and waited for the last tie-rod to be bolted in place or the last piling driven into the mud. Then they would head for whichever watering hole was closest to the job site, with Ernie and me following the two battered red *Gant and Seme* pickups in Ernie's 1934 Ford. That was my favorite car because it had a rumble seat and I felt like a king when I rode back there.

All four of the men in the crew were baseball fans, and they were initially in awe of Ernie, the former big leaguer, but eventually they became comfortable with him. They loved it when he had a few beers and would loosen up and tell stories about Babe Ruth, Ty Cobb, and Casey Stengel. I can't remember which teams they each rooted for, although my father was a Yankees fan, so my loyalties were torn between my father's Yankees and Ernie's Phillies. I was able to get around that because those teams were in different leagues, always wondering with great trepidation which team I would root for if the Yankees and the Phillies ever met in a World Series. Luckily for me, it only happened once, in 1950 when the Yankees, under Casey Stengel's leadership, beat the Phillies in four straight when I was only four-years-old. I was still a year away from my first game at a big-league ballpark.

And there was *no* way that Edie would have let Ernie expose me to my father's raunchy crew when I was four-years-old. It *was* close, because I was five the first few times. The usual argument among the crew when it wasn't about who the bustiest movie star or torch singer happened to be at that moment, was who is the greatest center-fielder now? Mantle, Mays, or Snider? Ernie's friend Richie Ashburn, also a Hall of Fame center fielder for the Phillies, didn't count. He was more or less an afterthought to those guys since New York baseball was all that mattered. Baseball was always the common denominator. So, my short season with Ernie begins with possibly my earliest memory of my time with him, and, of course, it's a baseball story.

That Skinny Number Nine

Ernie and I were already "having a catch" with a baseball almost daily when I was only four-years-old, my fifth birthday coming up in July of 1951. My brother Danny had been born in February, so while my mother was busy with him, I spent a lot of time in Philly with Ernie and Edie. I happened to be there a few days before my birthday and I remember hearing Edie telling Ernie, "He's still too young. He's still just a little boy."

I had no idea what they were "fratchen" about, as Edie used to say, but I quickly learned. Ernie was insistent. He was taking me to a ball game at Shibe Park for my birthday. The Red Sox and Ted Williams were in town playing against the A's. It was July 5, a night game, and I couldn't have been more excited. My birthday was still two days away.

Shibe Park, Philadelphia, Pa.
The Home of the Athletics

Anyone who doesn't remember his or her first game in a big-league ballpark is quite possibly dead or doesn't like baseball, or both. I would bet that most of my teammates, past and present, can tell you not only when and where they experienced a major league game in person for the first time, but also who was playing, and more often than not, who won the game, who pitched, what the score was, and who had the key hits. That doesn't even matter.

The first time you come up out of the dark tunnels under the stands (which they usually were in old ballparks) and into the bright lights, you see that emerald green grass for the first time and you *know* you've never seen greener grass. Then you see the scoreboard listing those other teams and games to be played, or scores of games in progress. You see the colorful advertising on the outfield fences and you hear the chatter of the players, the crack of the bat during batting practice, and you *know* also that it's a moment in your life you will never forget. It's like seeing the Grand Canyon, the Rocky Mountains, or the Eiffel Tower for the first time. And you never want that moment to end. For me, it never has.

That's how it was for me nearly 70 years ago, and I remember it like it was yesterday. Some things are still vivid, like the clouds of cigar smoke. Even now, when I smell a cigar, I think of that wonderful night in 1951. There were mostly men in the stands, most wearing suits and fedora hats, many wearing white shirts and ties. Vendors were yelling, "Hey, Getcha Scorecard here." And "Hey Hot Dog here," and of course, "Hey BEER here!" Lively organ music was playing. I had entered another world.

We found our seats, Pop Pop and me. The beer vendor found him, even calling him Mr. Padgett. People in nearby seats greeted him, many calling him Ernie. I was trying to watch batting practice and still take in everything that was going on around us at the same time. I was so excited I thought I might wet my pants, but I didn't. Ernie bought me a coke and a hot dog, but I was too excited to eat. So much was going on and I didn't want to miss any of it. So, *this* was what real baseball was all about!

There was kind of a screechy noise coming out of a big loudspeaker above our heads and a man read off a bunch of names and numbers and sometimes people cheered. A lot of people booed. One guy from the Red Sox got loud cheers and even louder boos. Some people came up and stood in front of me and asked Ernie to sign his name for them on their scorecards. I didn't understand why that happened back then, but he certainly did. And for some reason he thanked them. I do understand that now.

After that, all the players seemed to disappear from the field. Four umpires in black suits and funny looking black hats came out and stood by home plate. Two older looking men in uniforms, one gray and one white, came out of the dugouts and shook hands with each other along with the umpires, and they each gave the umpire who was holding a catcher's mask a piece of paper.

Ernie told me that was the home plate umpire and those older men in the white and gray uniforms were the managers. Those pieces of paper were called line-up cards. The line-up cards told the umpires who the players in the game were and their position in the batting order. Ernie said the game was almost ready to start. The two older guys went back to the dugouts. I already knew about dugouts. That's where the players went when they weren't on the field. It seemed like a great place to go if it rained.

The Red Sox, wearing gray uniforms, batted first, and while one batter was up another came out of the dugout swinging not one, but two bats. He knelt down inside a circle in the grass between home plate and the dugout and swung those bats. A tall skinny guy came out of the dugout with "9" on his back, with his hat kind of crooked on his head and he started swinging his two bats together. I knew that's how they warmed up before they went up to bat. Older guys in our neighborhood at home sometimes did that in our ball field next to the laundromat, where if you hit a ball into the dirty water that drained into left field, you were out. Ernie said that they swung two bats while getting ready to hit because when they dropped the bat they weren't going to use, the bat they *were* using felt lighter. That made sense.

I noticed that they spit a lot. I asked Ernie why, and he said it's because they chew tobacco. I said I didn't know you could *chew* tobacco. I thought you could only smoke it. Ernie just chuckled and ran his hand through my hair like he did sometimes. For some reason I really loved that. Other times he would just rest his hand on my head or on my shoulder and it made me feel special.

"Joey, you see that skinny Number '9' getting ready to bat?"

"Yes, Pop Pop. Who is that?"

"That's Ted Williams. He is the greatest hitter that ever lived and there will never ever be a greater hitter. He's also a great outfielder. I want you to watch him."

I said I would, and I did. At the time I didn't know what "loping" was, but I did notice that he had this loose, relaxed way of running and I heard people in the stands say that Williams "loped" when he ran. I also noticed that he could run pretty fast when he wanted to. And I never knew that anyone could smack a ball like he did.

Ted Williams went 3 for 5 in that game with a single, a double, and a home run. In the sixth inning he hit a line drive off a mediocre pitcher named Bob Hooper that I'm pretty sure was still rising when it cleared the high wall in right field at Shibe Park. To this day I remember the sound of it. The closest I can come to describing it would be the sound of the high-powered recoil-less rifle when I was a Marine, and I can still see it clearly in my mind as that ball disappeared into the Philadelphia night. The Red Sox won the game 8 to 3. I did see Ted Williams play several more times in Yankee Stadium, but nothing that he did stands out like that night, my first ballgame ever, in Philly with Pop Pop Ernie.

After the game Ernie and I slowly made our way toward the exit with the crowd. It was way past my bedtime, of course, but instead of leaving the ballpark, we turned a corner and started down a dark corridor toward what I realized was the locker room. As we passed the open door I saw some players still in their uniforms, some almost naked with towels wrapped around them. Men in suits and fedora hats with notebooks and pencils were talking to some players. There was a lot of smoke in there.

Ernie and I continued down the hall to an open door. Ernie knocked once and we walked into a large dimly-lit office with a lot of photographs on the walls. A tall white-haired old man in a three-piece suit and a flat-topped straw hat on his head was sitting at a large desk with his feet up. He was reading a newspaper but when he saw Ernie and me, he sort of unwound himself from his chair and stood up with a big smile on a very weathered face. My first thought was, "This guy is even older than Pop Pop. And a whole lot taller." At the time, that old man was already 89 years old.

"Ernie, it's so wonderful to see you. I haven't seen you in a long time. How are you?"

"I'm fine Connie." Ernie said, shaking the old man's hand. "How are you?"

"Not so well. Another tough loss tonight. Things are not going well this season. But we shall bounce back. We could use *you* out there right now, Ernie Padgett. Who's that you have there with you?"

I noticed that he said "thayah" instead of "there."

"Connie, I'd like you to meet my grandson, Joe. Joey, say hello to Connie Mack."

I shook his hand and said hello, thinking how huge his hand was and how very tall he was. And he talked kind of funny, like someone on the radio. He asked Ernie how Edith was doing, and if I was going to be a ballplayer.

"He's doing pretty good so far. We're working on it. I expect he'll grow some," Ernie said.

70

I noticed, and wondered why Connie Mack said "ball playah."

"That's a fine thing Ernie. I'm sure he will do well."

He turned to me and said, "You come back and see me sometime son, all right? Bring your Grandpa."

I said I surely would, but I was getting more tired by the minute and Ernie knew it. Ernie also knew he would have to answer to Edie for keeping me out so late. He and Connie Mack spoke for a few more minutes and we headed for the car. On the way, I asked him who that old man was.

"He's a great man, and I'll tell you all about him sometime soon. Someday you'll be proud to be able to tell *your* grandkids that you met him."

I'm sure I fell asleep in the car. Edie was waiting up for us and she asked if we had stopped at a tavern, but I knew she was kidding. As always, when I stayed with my grandparents, Ernie piggy-backed me up the stairs and Toby the bulldog and I went right to sleep despite his snoring and gas problems. I'm pretty sure I dreamed about baseball and "that skinny number '9'." I slept while Toby snored and snuggled under the covers with me. Life was good, and my birthday was still two days away.

Marty Marion & Connie Boswell

The next morning after Edie cooked a big breakfast, we loaded the car and headed from Philly to "the shore" and home for my birthday on Saturday. While he drove, Ernie told me that the old man I had met, Connie Mack, was born in 1862 and was the owner and former manager of the Philadelphia Athletics. He had been the manager for 50 years and now was the boss, no longer the manager. He was also among the first men inducted into the Hall of Fame.

I asked why he had a girl's name. Ernie chuckled and told me that when he was born, he was named Cornelius McGillicuddy, and what ballplayer would ever want a name like that?

I asked Ernie why Connie Mack talked funny. Edie chimed in that Connie Mack had been born in "Baaston and he paaked his cah in the yaad."

I had no idea what she was talking about. Ernie laughed so I did too, unsure why, I guess because I loved Edie.

I was up early for my birthday on Saturday, and saw a pile of colorfully wrapped presents on the table in our tiny kitchen. Norma was cooking eggs and bacon. Edie was coaxing my brother, "Baby Dan," to eat but he was focused on the pile of presents, oatmeal all over his face and pounding the tray of his high chair. My father and Ernie were drinking coffee, smoking and reading the papers. Ernie put down his paper and gestured to the pile of presents.

"What do you suppose this is all about?" he asked, his blue eyes twinkling.

"It's my birthday!"

"Ah!" said Ernie. "I thought it might be. And how old are you now, sixteen or seventeen?"

"I'm *five*," I said, looking at the wrapped boxes.

"Oh, that's right. I knew that," said Ernie.

My brother pointed at the presents, said something unintelligible, spitting out oatmeal.

"Breakfast first," my mother said.

I quickly shoveled in my eggs, gulped my juice and took a deep breath.

My eyes rested on a present that was about the size of a hat box, 'gift-wrapped' not with regular birthday wrapping paper, but with the colorful comics section of the Sunday paper, which was always Edie's idea of gift-wrapping. She handed me the box and told me it was from Nana and Pop Pop.

I already knew that from the wrapping paper, so I tore it off and opened the box. Inside was a brand new Spalding Marty Marion autograph model fielder's glove. In the pocket rested a new Spalding baseball. I couldn't believe it. As I was breathing in the smell of the new leather, my mother said something like, "Daddy, don't you think that's a little too big and too expensive for him now?"

I remember Ernie's response: "He'll grow into it. If he's going to be a ballplayer, he needs a proper glove. What do you say we go try it out?"

Ernie, my father and I headed for the back yard. Baby Dan started screaming. Edie told him he could go when he was a little bigger. She announced that she was pretty sure, based on the way he threw his toast across the room, he might indeed be a southpaw. He still is, but he plays ice hockey, not baseball. At one time he was a pretty decent first baseman, and he could hit. His problem was that when he got mad, which was common, he chased the other players with a bat.

My mother asked, "What about the other presents?"

"Later," I said, already out the door.

I have no idea what those other presents were, probably a bathing suit, new sneakers, and maybe a toothbrush. All I knew was that I now had a genuine Spalding. For years it was my proudest possession, mostly because it came from Ernie. We threw that new baseball back and forth nearly all that day until Ernie said he needed to sit down, and Edie brought him a beer. It was a great birthday.

A couple of days later, Ernie and I went to my father's job site on the river. I brought my new glove and showed it to the crew. They were impressed. Harry asked my father if he had a glove like that growing up. My father laughed and told us when he was a kid, he asked Grandpa John if he could have a baseball glove.

Grandpa John, who knew little about baseball replied, "Whatsa matta, you hands a get cold?"

The men laughed and turned their attention to teasing me. One of them said, "So we heard you met Connie Boswell at the ball game. You gonna tell us about her?"

I'm sure I looked puzzled because I had no idea who Connie Boswell was.

"She sure is a looker," said Jimmy. "Did she give you a big smooch? Man, I'd swim this river for a smooch from Connie Boswell."

I looked at Ernie and he had this special look that I recognized when he was amused, with the skin around his eyes kind of crinkled. It was what people are calling today 'smiling with your eyes.'

Ernie winked at me.

Harry asked me, "Did she sing a love song to ya? Ooh, I love ya so much, Joey baby! Gimme a kiss baby! Did ya get a date with her?"

"Hey," Jimmy said. "Does she got a sister? We can double date. Connie Boswell's got some *set* on her!"

I had no idea what he meant by a "set." A *set* of what? A *set* of tools like Ernie's? A *set* of dishes? I looked at Ernie and he winked at me again.

"Maybe she got *two* sisters," said Harry. "We can have a triple date. Hey Ernie, can we borrow the car? Joey and Connie can sit in the rumble seat."

"Yeah," said Jimmy, "We'll go to the drive-in and they can smooch!"

I was used to their teasing, but I was getting pretty flustered.

"Yeah," said Harry. "He can play with that *set*."

I had enough. I said, "I met *Connie Mack*. Not Connie Boswell. Pop Pop took me to meet him in his office after the game. He's in the Hall of Fame. I saw Ted Williams, the greatest hitter who ever lived, and he hit a home run. And what's a *set* anyway?"

75

They ignored my question.

"Who's he? Ted *who*? Is he a ballplayer?" asked Harry.

"Oh wait, I know; he plays a trumpet in Connie Boswell's band."

And they all laughed.

"You don't know what a *set* is? How old are ya anyway? Harry, tell him what a set is," said Jimmy.

"Okay 'shit kickers'," my father said. "Let's go back to work. This dock won't build itself."

"Kiss Connie for us," said Jimmy as he pulled on his heavy gloves and stepped back into the water.

"But be careful with that set!" said Harry. "Don't break it!"

Later, on the way to the bar, I asked Ernie who Connie Boswell was. He told me she was a singer and, in fact, she *really was* good looking and she *did* have two sisters who used to sing with her.

I said, "You better not tell Harry and Jimmy that. Hey Pop Pop, what's a *set*?"

He got that look in his eyes again and I think he was trying hard not to laugh.

"You'll know soon enough."

By then we were in the parking lot of the Red Lion; the crew was already inside.

"Come on," Ernie said. "I'm thirsty."

Crabs in the Kitchen

In the early 1950s Ernie was still working at Gibbs Underwear so he generally drove "down the shore" from Philly on Friday nights and returned on Sundays. Edie usually stayed in their cottage when he was in Philly, especially in the summer. I couldn't wait for Friday nights when Ernie would show up, bringing hoagies or Philly cheese steak sandwiches. Edie usually had a cold one waiting for him.

I always spent those weekends with them, sleeping on a scratchy old sofa with Toby on their screened porch. I would fall asleep while trying hard to stay awake, listening to Russ Hodges if a Giants game was on the radio, Mel Allen if it was a Yankees game, but most often Gene Kelly doing a Phillies game. Vin Scully did the Dodger games, but Ernie and I hated the Dodgers.

At some point, Ernie bought a black and white television with a tiny screen. It had a glass bubble that hung in front of the screen to magnify the picture, but it made me dizzy. Ernie still preferred to listen to the games on the radio while sitting on the porch with me, a cold beer in hand. Edie watched *The Jackie Gleason Show* through the glass bubble on the television in the living room.

They also had an old wooden rowboat, the *Norma Gloria*, named after my mother. In the winter it sat upside down on sawhorses in the yard with a canvas tarp over it. On some days my pals and I played soldiers at war under it.

In the winter, except for Christmas and occasional weekends, Edie and Ernie stayed in Philly and I would often visit them. I missed Toby, but not only that, it gave me a chance to get away from my brother Danny, who had begun following me around.

When spring came, Ernie would remove the tarp from the boat and patiently fold it and put it in the garage. Then he would bring out a can of gooey stuff called caulk. With my father's help, he would turn the boat over on the sawhorses and we carefully caulked all the cracks and joints. Then we added a fresh coat of paint and Ernie would grease the oarlocks.

"We don't want to sink, do we?" Ernie would say while we worked that sticky caulk into the cracks and joints. I certainly didn't want to sink, but secretly I thought that old boat *might* sink sometime.

When the caulking and paint were dry, Ernie and my father would load the boat into the bed of the red pickup, first removing any creosoted lumber that was still in the truck. We hauled the boat and the oars to what we called the "T Dock," at the end of Dock Road for the ceremonial launch. I rode in the back of the truck, in the boat. Sometimes when we were pulling out of the yard, Edie would offer to come with us and break a bottle of Cutty over the bow to christen the launch. We always declined. Even so, I don't think Edie wanted to waste good scotch and Ernie didn't want to scratch the paint, so it never happened.

With the *Norma Gloria* securely tied to the dock, my father drove us back to Edie and Ernie's. We always invited my father to go crabbing with us but he said he got enough sun and salt water during the week. We loaded the rumble seat with boat cushions, a basket with a lid for the crabs, carefully wound weighted lines, our dip net and a cooler that Edie packed. It was usually sandwiches, a Coke and maybe some cookies for me and a thermos of coffee and a couple of beers 'for later' for Ernie. Sometimes, either Edie or my mother slathered Coppertone all over me.

Growing up near the water, I already knew how to swim. The water wasn't very deep where we usually went, so we didn't bring a life jacket, against Edie and my mother's wishes. I think they knew Ernie would never let anything happen to me and they also knew the water at our usual spot was quite shallow. I did, however, find out a couple of years later that even shallow water can be dangerous.

We drove to the bait store for some smelly fish called moss bunkers which we cut into several pieces. Sometimes we stashed some of Toby's chicken livers in the basket for some variety for the crabs. Ernie said the smellier the better, although I didn't think crabs could smell anything under water. Toby was never invited on the expeditions. Ernie said he would get too hot and his farting might scare the crabs or make us want to jump out of the boat.

I thought that Toby could do what I did when I got hot, go swimming. I didn't push it since we were going crabbing, just Ernie and me. Little Danny was still too young and the few times we did take him with us he teased the crabs in the basket with a stick and he could never sit still, which Ernie said was important in a boat.

We always went crabbing early in the morning unless Ernie burned the breakfast and we stopped to eat at our favorite eatery, The Bazaar, a short walk down the street from the dock. Sonny, the cook, always reminded me when I was a little older, of the cook in the Beetle Bailey cartoons with his greasy apron and a lit cigarette dangling from his lip while he tended the grill. He would always ask me if Pop Pop burned our breakfast again. Ernie would always point at me. I was in on the joke by now, and I would just shrug; no big deal. I would have never told Ernie this, but I liked Sonny's eggs a whole lot better than his. Ernie's were either runny or burned.

Finally, we carefully loaded the boat and shoved off. People fishing or crabbing on the dock wished us luck. I would sit on the wide seat in the back of the boat while Ernie rowed. The oars creaked even though he always oiled the oarlocks. We never went very far from the dock because there was a long stretch of marsh grass close-by at the edge of the shallow water where the crabs liked to hang out. In truth, we probably could have caught just as many crabs if we stayed on the dock, but it was always more of an adventure in the boat. We anchored fifteen feet or so from the edge of the marsh.

We baited three or four lines with the moss bunker pieces or the chicken livers and carefully tossed them into the clear river water where they settled onto the white sandy bottom. Sometimes we could actually see the crabs sneaking up on the bait and tearing at it with their big scary claws. If the bait wasn't tied to the end of the line properly, the crabs would work it loose and skitter away with it. Most of the time I pulled in the lines, very slowly but steadily as Ernie taught me to do, and he would quickly, in one motion, catch the crab in a long-handled dip net and drop him (or her) in the basket. I quickly put the lid on it.

Sometimes there were two crabs on one chunk of bait and Ernie would net them both. Never far removed from baseball, we called that "hitting a double." I don't think we ever got a triple.

When the crabs were biting, Ernie sometimes pulled in the lines and he let me net them. I missed a few, but after a while I became pretty good at it and for many summers, we caught lots of big Jersey blue crabs. We never took more than we could eat. Ernie always said we needed to let some of the crabs go home to their families. That way there would be plenty of them left for next time, and other people could catch some.

Ernie wore an old Phillies cap but I was usually bareheaded, and in the summer my blond crew cut turned almost white. My friends called me "Whitey" sometimes. Sunburned and tired, Ernie rowed us back to the dock. There was a hose on the dock and Ernie insisted that we clean the boat before we left for home, washing out the moss bunker scales, crab slime, and leftover chicken liver parts.

Edie always greeted us at the kitchen door, her triumphant mariners now home from the sea. She would put a huge pot on the stove and start the water boiling. She added spices like paprika, red and black pepper, celery salt and vinegar, perhaps from one of Grandma Nellie's Cutty bottles while we waited for the water to boil. I'd like to think that maybe Nellie gave Edie a vinegar-filled Cutty bottle as a memento of Edie's

81

midnight tipple in Nellie's pantry. Probably not. Ernie would get a beer from the fridge, which Edie never failed to call the "icebox." Actually, it was more like an old icebox than today's modern refrigerators. Squatty looking with legs, it had one heavy door and there was always white ice, like a small glacier spilling out of the tiny freezer compartment. It had a large cylinder on top with a noisy motor inside.

I always hated the next part of the crab cooking ritual. Ernie would lift the basket and dump the live crabs, a few at a time into the boiling water. Even today, as much as I like to eat crabmeat, I wonder if crabs feel pain when they hit the water. Ernie said they didn't, and that God put crabs in the water so people could catch and eat them. I tried to believe him because I knew he'd never lie to me and they sure were good to eat.

Inevitably, when Ernie started to dump the crabs into the pot, some escaped, went scuttling across the linoleum kitchen floor and all hell broke loose. Toby barked and snapped at the crabs. The crabs snapped back, their pincers clicking. Some went under the icebox. Edie shrieked, "Get *that* one. No get the *other* one. He's going to bite my toes!"

I knew she wasn't serious but I went scrambling around anyway, barefoot, trying to catch the escapees without getting my toes or fingers pinched by those terrible claws. Ernie sat down at the kitchen table, sipped his beer and chuckled. Edie put her feet up on a chair and for or a split second I wondered if Ernie let some of the crabs escape on purpose. That might have been the most fun the three of us ever had together.

It seemed like every time we cooked crabs at least one last intrepid fighter wedged himself (or herself) in a corner under the cabinets, making one last stand like Davey Crockett at the Alamo, claws waving dangerously and no way for me to grab him (or her) from behind, with Toby barking furiously, while still keeping his distance. That crab was *not* going into the pot without a fight, dividing threats between Toby and me.

Having had lots of experience with this sort of thing, we knew what to do. I dropped a dish towel on the floor and the crab latched onto it. I pulled it out from under the cabinet, carefully grabbed the crab from behind so I wouldn't get my fingers pinched and dropped him (or her) into the pot, feeling quite guilty about it. If I had known that it was a "she" crab I would have felt even worse. Ernie reminded me how delicious crab meat tasted, dipped in melted butter or cocktail sauce and how wonderful Edie's crab cakes on a toasted bun were, and I felt better.

In the summer, Edie switched from Cutty Sark to gin and tonic during what she called "cocktail hour." My father said her cocktail hour lasted about 23 hours. Sometimes she let me taste her cocktail. I didn't exactly love it but it certainly tasted better than scotch. Once in a while she filled a glass with ice, tonic, and a slice of lime for me, and we sat under the big oak tree in the yard toasting each other and clinking glasses, waiting for the boiled crabs to cool a bit while we shucked some ears of corn for the pot.

Later, after a couple of cocktails and maybe a nap for Ernie, Toby and me, along with Norma, Danny and "Little Danny," we sat down to a crab feast in the yard at the picnic table. Edie had covered the table top with newspapers, and my father, who always liked to tease her, asked her if she wanted to save the now wet and sticky with crab juice comics section for gift wrapping since Christmas was only five months away. She stuck up her middle finger, which I knew was not a way to say thank you. My father's crew, his "shit kickers" did that all the time to each other.

Joe "The Barber"

In the early 1950s, Ernie and I attended many baseball games at Shibe Park. We saw the Philadelphia Athletics play lots of times until they moved to Kansas City after the 1954 season. I remember one game against the Tigers in which Bobby Shantz, the A's pitcher who was only 5 feet 6 inches tall and 140 pounds, pitched against the Tigers with his brother Wilmer "Billy" Shantz catching for the A's. It was almost like the "Ernie and Ralph" reunion in 1921. I couldn't believe that such a little guy like Bobby Shantz could be a pitcher. Billy Shantz only had one unspectacular year in the majors, like my Uncle Ralph in the minors.

The Tigers had future Hall of Famer Al Kaline and a pitcher with one of my all-time favorite names among ballplayers, Virgil Trucks. They also had a journeyman third baseman named Fred Hatfield who later became the baseball coach at my alma mater, Florida State. When I told Fred I saw him play once in Philly in the 50s, he looked at me for a few seconds, spit a stream of tobacco juice, said "No shit," and walked away. End of conversation. Fred knew baseball, but he was a man of few words.

We also saw a lot of Phillies games, Ernie and me. The Phillies bought Shibe Park from the A's when the latter departed for Kansas City and the ballpark was re-named Connie Mack Stadium. I never saw Connie Mack again. He died four years or so after I met him with Ernie in 1951.

Ernie was a Phillies fan, once in a while visiting the clubhouse, and he became friends with several of the players. Unfortunately, those visits were without me, but Ernie did bring me a ball autographed by the Phillies players, which I actually gave to the elderly father of one of my teammates who was dying of cancer, but a life-long Phillies fan. The last time I saw him, he thanked me with tears in his eyes.

During every game that Ernie and I enjoyed together it seemed like I learned something else about baseball. Ernie and I would sit side by side, our arms leaning on the railing in front of us and he would carefully point out and explain what was going on and why. He would tell me to watch the shortstop.

He was basically the boss of the infield and usually the best athlete. If the shortstop knew (and he always made it a point to know) for example, that a weak hitter, batting from the right side, usually couldn't pull a fastball to the left side of the infield (and the pitcher made it a point to know that also), the shortstop would "cheat" toward the middle of the diamond. If the batter was a power hitter who could pull the ball, he might cheat toward the left field line. Ernie stressed the importance of proper positioning.

Sometimes I would spot something going on and I would ask him about it. I wondered why, for instance, with a man on first base, before the pitch, the shortstop would cover his mouth with his glove so only the second baseman could see it. Ernie told me that was how they determined who would cover second on an attempted steal: Mouth open: "You cover." Mouth closed: "I'll cover."

86

There was so much to learn, much more than hitting or catching the ball. There were the third base coach's signals, the catcher's signals for what pitches he wanted the pitcher to throw, and how they had to change the signals with a runner on second base who might possibly steal the signs and relay to the batter what pitch is coming. I sometimes felt like I'd never be able to grasp it all, but in time and with Ernie's patient explanations, I learned. And like most every ballplayer, I'm always learning, even after seven decades on the field.

Ernie also explained to me what are called the "Cardinal Rules of Baseball." These are unwritten rules, none are in the official rule books, but every good player knows them. A few: Never make the first or third out at third base; never throw at a batter's head; always hit the cut-off man; always take the first pitch if the batter in front of you walks on four straight pitches; never take a close pitch with two strikes; never try to intentionally injure another player. There are more, and they become second nature to most ballplayers.

My father attended some games with us before the A's left for Kansas City, often when the Yankees were in Philly. Later, all three of us watched a lot of games in Yankee Stadium. We saw nearly every major league team and I was especially excited the first time I saw the Yankees in '52 or '53. Joe DiMaggio had retired after the 1951 season, so I never saw him play in person but my guy was Mickey Mantle.

I started collecting baseball cards in 1952 and I know I had at least 10 "Topps '52 Mantle" cards. A Mint condition '52 Topps' Mantle card can sell today for hundreds of thousands of dollars or more. Like most men of my generation with the same sad story, my mother threw my baseball cards away when I went off to college. Thanks Mom. I never wanted to retire anyway.

MARCH, 1953

Ernie

Ernie was still working for Gibbs Underwear when I was five or six, and when I was visiting in Philly he used to bring home some of the heavy cardboard cones that held the yarn for the giant looms at the factory, or as Ernie always said, "the mill." These cones were about a foot long, about 4 inches wide at the bottom and each one had a shiny colored tip that matched the color of the yarn that had been on the cone. The empty cones were thrown away, and Ernie used to bring a few home for me to play with. You can't actually build anything with cones, so I used to line them up in different patterns and knock them down with a baseball (rolling the ball like bowling; not throwing it). Edie had a lot of breakables.

I also liked to tease my pal Toby the bulldog when I was bored. Sometimes when he was sleeping, I built a fence around him with the cones. I would hide somewhere nearby and make "meow" sounds like a cat. Toby didn't like cats since a couple of neighborhood cats would sit outside the window, driving him crazy. When he heard me, he would jump up and knock the cones down, ready to chase the cats. We would say, *"Get those Cats,"* and he would run from room-to-room barking, looking for them. Realizing he had been duped, he'd get a kind of pissed off look on his face and leave the room, dignity intact. However, Toby, like most bulldogs, always looked somewhat pissed off.

The most fun I had at Edie and Ernie's, other than going to the ballpark with Ernie, was when I opened my "barber shop." Ernie painted two of the cones white and added a red spiral stripe to each one like a barber pole. He also painted a small sign for me with a red frame around it that read "Joe's Barber Shop."

I would be all ready for him when he came home in the afternoon. He would remove his suit coat and carefully hang it up, loosen his tie, unbutton his vest and lie back in his recliner. By then, Edie would have brought him a beer. I don't remember if he drank gin and tonic.

Someone had given me a plastic toy barber shop set, probably for my birthday. It had clippers that couldn't cut anything, a comb and brush, hand mirror, a mug and brush for shaving cream, a plastic straight razor and a wide brush with a small dust pan for sweeping up imaginary clippings. Edie supplied a sheet and Ernie provided an old leather belt for a razor strop. I already had my sign and barber pole cones set up on the table next to Ernie's chair. "Joe's Barber Shop" was open for business. I would spread the sheet over Ernie and tuck it inside his collar, the same way Tony the barber did at his one-chair shop in our neighborhood at home. The only difference was that I didn't provide comic books for my one and only customer.

Once I tried to entice Edie into letting me work on her hair but she said she didn't want me to disturb her glamorous permanent wave and spoil her movie star beauty. That was okay with me because she had thick kinky hair which might have broken my comb. I certainly didn't see her as a movie star. She was always plain old Nana or Edie to me, thick in the middle and getting creaky. Toby always ran when he saw my clippers. They weren't battery powered, so I supplied the buzzing noise. He ran away anyway.

Sheet in place, I messed up Ernie's red and now graying hair with my fingers. I buzzed him with my clippers, carefully combing as I went along just like Tony did. I supplied the noise, speeding up and slowing down the buzz as necessary. By now Toby was back in the room watching carefully, knowing he was safely off the hook for a while. Finished with the clippers, I combed Ernie's hair. Sometimes I parted it down the middle and held up the mirror for his approval. If he didn't like that look, I parted it on the side (knowing it was the wrong side) and held the mirror up again. He didn't like that either. Finally, I got it right and carefully combed it so it looked pretty much like it did when he sat down.

I lathered his face, usually with imaginary shaving cream but using the brush anyway. I would always tickle his nose with the brush and he would do a couple of fake sneezes. Once in a while I was allowed to use real shaving cream that I carefully stirred in the mug. I used the leather belt to 'strop' my plastic straight razor and I carefully scraped the shaving cream off his face, wiping my razor on a towel. I always wiped the towel even when I used make-believe shaving cream. I would slap some Old Spice on his cheeks, the same way Tony did it, and I'd hold up the mirror. Satisfied, Ernie reached into his vest pocket, paid me a quarter with a nickel or dime tip, and it was time for supper.

Ernie Shot an Eagle

The first time that I remember seeing Ernie drunk, or "feeling no pain" as he referred to it, was once when he came home from playing golf with his buddies. They had stopped at their favorite tavern on the way home and Ernie was in the mood to celebrate. He had shot an eagle during the round, scoring a three on a par five hole. It was a first for him and a reason to celebrate.

He came through the door happily dragging his heavy old brown leather golf bag, looking a lot less dignified than I was used to seeing. He shook my hand, pumping it vigorously. I never remembered him doing that before. He gave me a hug. That was no surprise because he did that a lot. Then he gave Edie a hug, lifting her off the floor, which could not have been easy.

His first words were, "*Ede*, I shot an *Eagle!*"

I didn't think you were allowed to shoot eagles. And why would an eagle be on a golf course? I was confused and kind of disappointed that Pop Pop would do such a thing.

"Ern, you're *drunk!*"

She shook her head.

"Nice example."

That was also rather confusing. It wasn't like I had never seen *her* drunk. "Tipsy," she used to say.

"Hell *yeah,* I am," he said. "A *three* on a par *five!* Damn *right!* That's a reason to celebrate. It was *fifty* yards out, maybe more, and it went *right* into the *hole!* I never hit a baseball that good!"

He scratched his head and continued, "Well, maybe that *one* time in Forbes Field in '25. I hit the *shit* out of *that* ball!"

I was still thinking about the possibly dead eagle. "What does that *mean*, Pop Pop?" I wanted to know. "Did you really shoot an eagle?"

He ruffled my hair.

"No, 'course not. See, in golf you get so many shots on each hole. That's called *par*. There are eighteen holes. Each hole has a different par. A *par five* hole means you gotta try to put the ball in the hole in five tries counting from when you tee off. If it takes you more than five on that hole, that's called 'over par.' If it takes less, that's called 'under par.' If you make the hole in four shots on a par five, that's called a 'birdie.' You see?"

"But what about the eagle?" I said, still flustered. "Did you kill him?"

Ernie smelled awful, like beer, sweat and cigar smoke.

"No. Nobody killed an eagle. An 'eagle' is what it's called when you make it in two strokes under par. That's what I did. Never did that before. I didn't shoot an actual eagle. Besides, I don't have a gun in my golf bag, and you know I wouldn't do that, don't you?"

I felt a little better; no dead eagle. Crabs were one thing but eagles were something else.

"Kind of like your triple play?" I asked. I knew all about his triple play.

"Zackly. Close anyway. Mostly luck."

He sprawled out in his recliner and was soon snoring. Toby looked at me as if to say, "See, I'm not the only one who snores."

I sat down near Ernie, looked at Toby, and he jumped up in my lap.

Edie gently removed Ernie's shoes and went to the kitchen to finish cooking supper.

It wasn't long after that when I started getting hints that Ernie might be sick. I heard bits of phone conversations between Edie and my mother.

"And so, what did the doctor *say*?" And, "When do they want to see him again?" And, "Well is *that* what's causing the pain?"

I sometimes heard the words "X-ray" and "surgery." I was maybe six-years-old at the time, and all I knew was that he had a sore leg which he always told me was nothing to worry about.

So, I didn't worry about it. I forgot about it.

For a while.

Get that Damn Doctor
Back Out Here

By now it probably seems like I spent a lot of time in Philly with Edie and Ernie, usually for a few days at a time when Ernie wanted to take me to a ball game or an occasional weekend in the winter. In the summer, Edie and Toby stayed in their cottage down the street from us, and I did spend a lot of time with them, although I didn't like to be there when Edie was cooking Toby's chicken livers.

When Ernie came for the weekends or when he had some vacation time, we worked on my baseball instruction. We would go to our rustic, rock-strewn and often muddy ball field next to the old laundromat, or to a narrow vacant lot next to our house. When we played there, a lot of windows were broken. There was a picnic table for when Ernie needed to sit down to rest.

He would pitch to me, teaching me to hit the ball to all fields. I was still pretty small like he was and he told me I would be a "slap hitter," which is what he was called when he played. He also taught me to bunt and not to swing at bad pitches. At other times we would throw the ball back and forth in the back yard, working on short hops and keeping my head down. Ernie explained that if you turned your head away when fielding a ball, you stood a better chance of getting hit in the face than if you kept your head down and never took your eye off the ball. Sometimes it's hard to remember that while trying to glove a hard sinking liner with a lot of top-spin that you have to short hop on your backhand side.

During some of those practice sessions I started to notice that Ernie tired quickly and sat down more frequently. I also noticed that he coughed a lot. He said it was summer allergies so I never worried about it. Once in a while I would think about those strange phone conversations I heard from time to time. Who were they talking about? Was Pop Pop sick? It was summer and baseball season, and I pushed that out of my mind. A lot of the time he sat at the picnic table, watching and giving advice.

Most of our summer days while Ernie was in Philly and my father was working were spent at the beach. We loaded Edie's old Ford with blankets, towels, and a cooler and headed to the ocean, my brother Danny and me happily riding in the rumble seat. Mostly, we walked to our local beach on the Metedeconk River. My mother pushed Danny's stroller while I tried not to burn my bare feet on the hot pavement, hopping from one shady spot to the next. Flip flops hadn't been invented yet. I couldn't wait to hit that water and cool my feet. As soon as the woman at the gate checked our 1952 membership badges, I ran to the water.

Little Danny, as we now called him (although some people still called him "Baby Dan"), now two-and-a-half-years old, was already a handful, full of energy and always into some kind of mischief. He also wanted to be in the water with me, so of course I had to watch him to make sure he was safe. The water at the edge of the beach was shallow, a foot deep at most. A lifeguard, usually a teenager, was on duty, but like most teenage lifeguards, he spent more time watching the girls on the beach strutting back and forth to the snack bar than watching the swimmers, in those days called "bathers." Edie used to say in that Philly accent of hers, "We're gawn bathin." Dogs were allowed on the beaches in those days and Toby often came with us.

As eager as we were to get wet, my mother usually made us wait for that designated and somewhat mythical *one hour* after eating breakfast before we could go into the water. I spent the time hopping from one foot to the other on the hot sand while pointing out to her that the water was less than a foot deep and we weren't actually going *swimming*. She was probably tired of Danny whining anyway, and after a while she let us go. On this day, for some reason, Edie and Toby had stayed home. Edie certainly would have enforced the one-hour rule.

In the water now, we had a rubber raft with a pull rope attached and another rope running through grommets on the sides to hang onto. Danny had a plastic inner tube around his waist and he was holding the rope at the back of the raft. I was pulling the raft through the shallow water as fast as I could, making motor boat sounds, not unlike the sounds I made when using my clippers on Ernie's hair. Danny was laughing. I was laughing in-between making motor boat noises.

My mother was sitting on a beach chair about twenty feet away, watching us closely while chatting with her friends who also had kids playing in the shallow water.

Danny and I were having a great time with "Joe the motor boat" pulling him along. I didn't see it and I don't know how, but it happened quickly. Danny toppled upside down and was tangled in the rope on the end of the raft. He had been laughing happily and then his laugh changed, then stopped altogether. He had been trying to pull himself up and was gasping for air, not laughing as I thought.

Suddenly, it was very quiet, like a suspension in time. I glanced at my mother and saw a look of horror on her face. She was on her feet, running toward us. I looked back and saw Danny's little legs and feet sticking out of the now upside-down inner tube. He was ensnared in the rope with his head and upper body under water, not moving.

Before I could do or say anything, my mother scooped him up and ran back to shore. By now there was panic on the beach; people were screaming. The lifeguard came running, told someone to go inside the snack bar and call an ambulance. They laid Danny face down on a blanket and began lifting his arms up and down, pushing on his back. In those days they called it artificial respiration. Some water dribbled out of his mouth but he still didn't move. A man came running out of the snack bar and said the rescue squad was close-by, on the way. I was terrified and shivering. Someone wrapped a towel around me. I was thinking how tiny Danny was.

Kathy, a nurse who was a friend of my mother's, pushed the frightened lifeguard out of the way and kept working on Danny, gently pushing down on his tiny back and lifting his arms. She kept saying, "Come on Danny. You can do it. *Breathe!*"

It seemed like forever, but we could hear the siren in the distance. I kept saying to anyone who might listen, "It was an *accident,* I didn't *mean* it!" A woman said something like, "Of course it was; of course, you didn't," and put her arm around my shoulders.

In a few more minutes two men and two women in white coveralls were running across the beach carrying a stretcher. One was carrying an oxygen tank and a small machine. They immediately turned Danny over, clamped a mask on his face and started to give him oxygen. More water dribbled out of his mouth. He still didn't move. One of the rescue squad women pushed gently on his chest. They lifted him onto the stretcher and ran to the ambulance, still giving him oxygen with the woman holding the tank running alongside the stretcher. My mother and I were close behind. As we ran, she told Kathy to call Edie and Ernie to let them know, and somehow get word to my father. Ernie would know where he was working.

She had grabbed her beach robe, sandals, and beach bag. All I had was the towel wrapped around my shoulders, and I was barefoot. The two attendants, one man and one woman, loaded Danny's stretcher into the back of the ambulance. My mother and I clambered in after them.

The other two attendants jumped into the front of the ambulance and soon we were rolling, siren wailing. The woman covered Danny with some blankets and kept the oxygen mask on his face while the man monitored the gauges. Danny was turning blue. I kept thinking that he was going to get those blankets all wet. We could hear the attendant in the front of the ambulance on the radio, telling someone at the hospital that they were on the way with a little boy "drowning victim." Please be ready.

When my mother heard that, she let out a low moan. I kept saying I was sorry and that it was an accident. She put her arm around me and said she knew that. It didn't make me feel better because I might have killed my baby brother. I kept seeing those little legs and feet sticking out of the water.

I couldn't stop shivering. It was cold in the ambulance and my bathing suit and towel were both wet. I wondered whose towel I had. They would probably want it back, though I noticed that one corner was frayed. There were little pools of water and a lot of sand on the floor as well as on my feet. My mother had sand on her ankles. One sandal was unbuckled, the strap hanging loose, her hand resting on Danny's tiny foot which was sticking out of the blanket and now pale blue. I knew she was terrified. I was beyond terrified.

On the way to the hospital, I looked around inside the ambulance and at the two white-clad people who were working to save Danny. The woman was soft and kind looking with a white military-style cap on top of her silvery white hair. I realized she was pretty old. She held the oxygen mask on Danny's face, smoothing his hair with her other hand, sometimes patting my mother on the knee. With a gentle smile, she kept telling my mother it will be all right.

The man working the dials on the oxygen resuscitator was her husband. He also had silver hair and wore a white baseball cap with a red cross on it. He had a patch on his coveralls with lettering that read *Community First Aid*. Once or twice, he winked at me as if to say, "It will be okay." I wasn't so sure.

Later I learned that their names were Tully and Walt Sittig. They soon became my mother's close friends and mentors, and they were working hard to save my brother's life.

When we reached the hospital, a doctor and a nurse were waiting in the parking lot. My mother and I climbed out of the ambulance as the doctor and the nurse squeezed in. The doctor listened to Danny's chest with his stethoscope while the nurse felt his wrist and shook her head. The doctor said there was nothing that he could do; this little boy is too far gone. My mother screamed, "NO!"

The doctor said he was very sorry, told Tully and Walt to bring him inside the hospital. They didn't. Walt turned up the dials and Tully pushed on Danny's chest, her kind smile now gone. Her face was grim. My mother and I stood in the parking lot, watching in horror.

I know the word today but I didn't then. The word is "surreal," and I remember it like it was yesterday. I have no idea today what that doctor looked like. I only heard what he said, "This little boy is too far gone. We can't save him."

Tully and Walt kept working. Walt kept saying, "Come on boy. Come on boy." All of a sudden Danny coughed and water poured out of his mouth onto the floor of the ambulance. He coughed again and more water poured out of his mouth, this time all over the blankets. There was white foamy stuff in the water.

"*Walt*," Tully yelled. "Get that *damn* doctor out here again!"

Walt headed for the door. The two attendants from the front seat, another older couple, were already in the back of the ambulance lifting the stretcher, putting down the wheels and heading for the door to the Emergency Room. My mother and I followed Tully. The doctor and several nurses quickly wheeled Danny's stretcher into a room and closed the door behind them. We stood watching through a thick glass window. I could see that Danny was moving his legs. I heard my mother say, "Oh, Thank God."

Edie soon arrived, having sent Ernie to find my father. I noticed that her permanent wave was not looking so great. She didn't look like a movie star now. When my mother told her what the doctor had said, Edie said she would kill him, then she thought better of it when she realized that my father probably would do it instead. I was worried about that when my father and Ernie showed up at the hospital a few minutes later. Ernie was driving his car and my father was following in his red pickup. He was in his work clothes, cut-off jeans, work boots and a sleeveless sweatshirt covered with creosote. I remember thinking how big his muscles were. My mother ran and hugged him. I thought she might get creosote on her beach robe, but she didn't care.

Edie and Ernie just looked at each other. I had never seen Ernie look frightened before. Whoever called Edie must have told her to bring us some dry clothes, which she did. However, it was a long time before I stopped shivering. Ernie put his arm around me.

The doctor came into the waiting room acting like suddenly he was our best buddy. He told us Danny was doing well, saying, "the little guy gave us quite a scare." I was thinking it's a good thing, because Big Danny would have done more than just scare that doctor. I was glad that he didn't have to.

They admitted Danny to the hospital and kept him in an oxygen tent for a couple of days, "under observation" they called it. They were worried about possible brain damage from oxygen deprivation, but he was fine. Of course, I often tell him that I wonder about that. His response is always, "Well, you tried to drown me."

Danny the Menace

The scary near-drowning incident brought two major changes to our lives. About a week after Little Danny came home from his stay in the hospital, my mother promptly joined the *Community First Aid Volunteer Rescue Squad*. She immediately started taking training classes. She felt that was the least she could do to show her appreciation for them saving Danny's life.

As the years went by, she became the captain of the squad and she held that position for close to two decades. For several years we had a direct hot-line from the police station to our home, and another direct line to the squad headquarters. An elderly couple lived in an apartment above the ambulance bays. When they got the call from Norma, the siren on the tower above the building immediately came to life, waking everyone within a half mile radius. Soon the volunteers, most of whom lived close-by, were on their way to try to save lives.

My mother also became the "go-to" medical person in our neighborhood when someone, usually a kid, sliced open a finger or stepped on a nail. Later, in mid-life, my mother went through training and became an emergency room nurse and worked well into her seventies.

The other major change in our lives had more direct impact on our family and the neighborhood, and not always in a good way. I bore much of the brunt of it. Danny, having survived drowning, could do or get away with almost anything. My mother said he was *delicate*, which he certainly was not. He made Dennis the Menace look like a choir boy. In fact, people in the neighborhood started calling him "Danny the Menace," for good reason.

He became more and more fearless as he grew, showing off for the neighborhood kids who constantly encouraged him. They came up with all sorts of outrageous stunts for him to attempt. My mother found him on the roof several times with no idea how he got up there. He climbed to the tops of trees and sometimes he would dangle upside down. Once he jumped from the roof of a house under construction, using an umbrella as a parachute, much to the delight of the gang who

Norma

cheered him on. My mother heard the shouting, came running, yelling at him. He jumped anyway. Of course, the umbrella collapsed in mid-jump, luckily, he landed in a sand pile, uninjured this time. Other times he wasn't so lucky and he endured well over 100 sutures, often five or six at a time before he was ten-years-old.

Along with his pal Alan, he set the woods at the end of our street on fire, hiding under Alan's front steps while the fire department extinguished the blaze. Some neighbors had seen them running out of the woods, with smoke billowing behind them. They denied it, but once they were separated, under questioning by the cops, they each blamed the other. The next day they were best buddies again.

Danny teased cats, dumped trash cans, broke windows. Our parents were on a first-name basis with the local juvenile officer, Murray Nesselbaum. He would show up at our house with a uniformed state trooper to try to scare Danny. They threatened to take him away to juvenile hall; it didn't matter. Soon he was being blamed for anything bad that happened in the neighborhood whether he did it or not.

To be fair, he usually did whatever he was accused of. Once he was blamed for vandalism that took place while we were in Philly visiting Edie and Ernie. It made my mother happy to be able to tell Officer Nesselbaum that *this* time Danny wasn't responsible. We all knew that most of the time he was. How could anyone blame this angelic looking little boy with those big blue eyes?

Several times my mother actually started to pack Danny's suitcase, making a big show of it and telling him she was taking him to the juvenile home herself. She said if he was going to be a bad boy he might as well go to live with other bad boys and that they *whipped* the bad boys there. That didn't scare him either.

He would beg and plead with my mother and promise to be a good boy until she gave in, putting his suitcase away, usually leaving it packed *just in case*. Then he would get this sly look on his face, knowing he got away with it again. I actually hoped she *would* take him to juvenile hall because I knew it would make my life a lot easier.

Ernie thought he could get Danny interested in baseball, and started including him in our practices. He bought him a glove, and of course Danny left it at the ball field. My father sent him back to get it. When he came back, my father asked him if he found his glove. Danny told him he didn't find his glove but he said he found something better. He opened his hands to show us a maggoty dead Blue Jay.

My mother washed his clothes with trepidation. Going through his pockets, she found live lizards or frogs, a dead mouse or an occasional dead snake. One day an evil smell was emanating from under Danny's bed. It was a bloated dead possum, so swollen that we had to lift the bed to remove it.

His most famous stunt took place early in his first year in kindergarten. I was in third or fourth grade at the time, so we rode the same bus to school. About a dozen kids waited with us at the bus stop, a short walk from our house. There was a dead skunk in the middle of the road, already quite fragrant in the early morning September sunshine.

To entertain the kids at the bus stop, Danny danced on the dead skunk. The bus came and we piled on, and I knew it was going to be a bad day. On the way to school the bus driver got sick and several kids threw up. The teacher/bus monitor at the school would not let Danny into the building. Someone called the principal. There was no way to let him into the classroom and nobody volunteered to drive him home, so they had no choice but to let him walk.

There was a path that we called the skinny path, a ten-minute walk to our house through a patch of woods that by now had mostly recovered from the fire. We walked home from school a lot, and Danny knew the way. I was delegated to accompany him to make sure he made it home safely. I walked at a fair distance behind him and tried to stay upwind. I knew that all hell would break loose when we reached home.

When we arrived, my mother was upset to say the least. Ernie was dispatched again to tell my father to come home. Edie and my mother stripped Danny of his skunk-ripe clothes and dropped them into the backyard trashcan to be burned.

According to Edie, normal soap would not work to remove skunk-smell from skin. Tomato juice was the answer, so Danny stood naked in the yard while Edie went to get tomato juice. It occurred to me much later, upon hearing this story for the umpteenth time, that somewhere along the way Edie had expanded the horizons of cocktail hour with a Bloody Mary, so there was tomato juice in her kitchen cupboards. I think Ernie also drank it with breakfast.

Edie was giving Danny a tomato juice bath when my father and Ernie showed up. My father was not happy, having to leave work early in the day. He began swearing in Italian as he sometimes did when he was mad. He was *really* mad. This time Danny got a spanking and was sent to his room, except for days afterward we sometimes got a whiff of skunk and tomato juice. Of course, I was asked why I let him do his skunk dance. I *let* him do it? Really?

"After all," they said, "you're his big brother and you should be looking out for him."

Yeah. Right.

The first time Danny went with us to a game at Yankee Stadium we had great box seats in the upper deck behind home plate. Danny and I sat in the front row, a low concrete wall in front of us and a rail about a foot above it. We could see everything. Ernie and my father sat behind us. I was watching Whitey Ford's incredible curve ball and not paying attention to Danny. I assumed that he was watching the game and enjoying his first time at *The Stadium*, as most Yankee fans called it.

It was maybe the third inning. We were taken by surprise when a cop came down the aisle and lifted Danny out of his seat by his collar. We thought he had been watching the game, but he had been leaning under the railing, spitting and dribbling Coke on the people below. It took some fast talking by my father and Ernie to keep us from being thrown out of the stadium.

Like everything else that Danny was involved in, it happened quickly. Ernie probably told the cop that he and Casey Stengel had been teammates in 1924. I was worried about not getting to see Mickey Mantle bat again and I didn't get the feeling that the cop believed Ernie.

A New York cop has heard it all, and his response was probably something like, "Sure buddy. And Babe Ruth was my uncle. Yuz guys are in trouble!"

My father went downstairs and apologized to the people Danny had spit on, buying beer and hot dogs for a few dampened fans. The cop let us off the hook. Anyone who has ever been to a Yankees game knows that New York fans are not exactly the most laid-back fans in baseball. But hey, free beer might be worth a little kid spit on the top of your head. It was quite a while before Danny was invited to go to another game. Besides that, there was still plenty of mischief left to be done in the neighborhood.

I mentioned before that Ernie and I built things in his basement workshop in Philly. I also built elaborate sailing ship models at the desk in my room at home. With Ernie's help, using thread and toothpicks with dabs of glue, I carefully made rope ladders and rigging. We also spent hours working on the sails, guns, and lifeboats. I painted tiny sailors perched in the crow's nests, manning the cannons or scrubbing the decks. Even back then, I painted a lot of detail. (I still do, but my eyes were better then.) Many of these ship models took weeks to complete while it took Danny only a matter of seconds to destroy them.

Of course, he always batted his blue eyes at us and swore it was an accident. He didn't *mean* to hit that ship with a bat or drop that cinder block on it. Occasionally, one of the neighborhood kids would give him a firecracker or a cherry bomb even though he wasn't allowed to have matches. He would take these beautiful, meticulously-crafted ship models outside and blow them up, always with an audience. Of course, I was never around. That too was only an *accident*. He never knew how that cherry bomb got into that ship, or who lit that fuse. I simply wanted to kill him, and there were those momentary thoughts about that day at the beach... .

I wasn't allowed to touch him. I hate to admit this and I still get teased about it, but I got *so* mad one time that I actually chewed the front edge of the top of my dresser, working my way across the wood like I was eating corn on the cob, leaving teeth marks on the wood. I was punished but Danny wasn't, despite having blown up the *USS Constitution* or the *Mayflower*. As usual, I was confined to my room. Danny peeked in, sticking his tongue out. After all, he had almost drowned.

In a recent conversation with Danny, he told me he found the bill for his hospital stay on July 28-29, 1952 in a box of old papers. An X-ray was $8.00. The total bill was $27.00. When he asked me for the hundredth time how the wood on the top of my dresser tasted, I asked him how the Metedeconk River water tasted.

Superman Christmas

Christmas in the early 1950s was always a special time for us. We normally didn't see Edie and Ernie for several weeks before the holidays. We knew Ernie would be busy in his basement workshop in Philly, creating something wonderful for us. He loved model railroads, and I was probably two or three when he bought me my first set of trains in 1948 or 1949. They were A.C. Gilbert *American Flyers,* with a steam locomotive, coal tender, freight cars, and caboose. I still have them.

As much as he loved the actual trains, Ernie loved to create the layout. He started with a sheet of plywood set on sawhorses in our porch/dining room. He drilled holes in the plywood and ran a string of lights underneath with a bulb poking up though each hole. After that, he laid down sheets of cotton *snow* fastening the tracks to the platform with tiny screws. Over each light bulb he placed miniature houses, stores, fire stations and other structures, most of which he built and painted himself, all matching the scale of the trains. There was also an old tin train station that had belonged to my late Uncle Joe back in the 1930s. It was the only thing on the platform that didn't fit the scale, but it didn't matter. That station still sits on a shelf in my sun room with the *American Flyers.*

Ernie built and painted a miniature picket fence to surround the whole layout. He added cars and trucks, miniature people, lead farm animals, for some reason mostly pigs. The Christmas tree sat in the middle of the layout. On Christmas morning, it was all magic. Later on, I wondered if Ernie did all that for us or for himself, or maybe for Uncle Joe. I do know that when he lovingly placed that wonderful old train station on the platform it was a bittersweet moment for him, as well as for Edie and my mother. There are still today decades-old wisps of cotton snow inside that station.

Christmas Eve back then was also special. Edie and Ernie would show up early in the day, along with my pal Toby, who was always excited to see me and vice versa. Ernie would work on the train layout while my mother visited with Edie as she cooked, usually some kind of hearty stew.

My father, happy that he wasn't freezing his ass off somewhere in the cold December water of Barnegat Bay working on some summer boater's dock, read the newspaper. If it happened to be around 1953 or 1954, he might have been watching a football game on our new black and white TV. I was always torn between watching football with my father, playing with Toby, or helping Ernie set up the trains. Most of the time, game or no game, my father sat and chatted with Ernie while he worked, usually about baseball. It was always (and still is) a source of pride for me to know how much love and respect these two men had for each other despite being so different, yet alike in so many ways. I stayed close to Ernie also, handing him a screwdriver or a pair of pliers while he worked on the wiring under the train platform, lying on his back with a beer close by. Since it was now winter, Edie was back with her old pal Cutty on the rocks.

I noticed that Ernie had more frequent coughing fits. He said it was from the attic dust on the train boxes. He also wriggled out from under the table and went into the bathroom a lot. I always thought that was because he drank a lot of beer.

"Danny the Menace" could not sit still. For about a week he had been battling Mumps, a childhood malady that caused painful swelling of the salivary glands, thus swollen cheeks. A vaccine was still ten years or more away. Maybe it was coincidental, maybe it had something to do with being in the hospital after nearly drowning, but Danny seemed more susceptible to childhood diseases than most kids. When he wasn't jumping off a roof, setting fires, or hanging upside down in a tree he was often sick.

Mumps didn't slow him down; painful swollen cheeks be damned. He would rip open the boxes containing the locomotive and freight cars, pushing the locomotive and train cars along the floor, chasing Toby. He lined up the farm animals and knocked them down. Edie suggested that he should have a nap, but he wasn't buying that.

"No Nana. No nap."

"Then behave yourself. Or Santa won't be bringing you anything but a lump of coal."

His blue eyes widened. "Yes, Nana."

I think if he knew how to use his middle finger back then, he would have happily shown it to Edie.

By suppertime, the train layout was ready for a trial run. My mother announced, "Supper first." Ernie winked at me and said we should wash our hands. Then we sat down to eat.

Danny was quiet, possibly thinking about that lump of coal and all the things he could damage with it.

After supper, Ernie and my father watched the news on our new black and white TV while Edie and my mother cleaned up the kitchen. After the news, Ernie and I plugged in the transformer 'control central' and put the train through a trial run. He showed me how to slow the train down on the curves and how to speed it up on the straight stretches by moving the lever on the transformer up or down.

Of course, Danny had to be the engineer also, and before anyone could stop him, he increased the speed on the curves instead of on the straightaway. The locomotive and freight cars careened sideways off the tracks, breaking through Ernie's meticulously crafted picket fence and landing on the floor. Ernie was not pleased, but as always, he maintained his cool.

Edie, not so much.

She picked Danny up and parked him in front of the TV in the living room, reminding him about the lump of coal while I tended to the train wreck and Ernie set about repairing the fence.

Meanwhile, *Superman* was now on the TV. George Reeves, a.k.a., Clark Kent, was in the process of being faster than a speeding bullet, leaping tall buildings in a single bound, and getting ready to rescue Lois Lane (usually bound and gagged) from despicable but inept kidnappers. Inevitably, one of them usually went sailing through an open window without benefit of a cape.

Danny was entranced and sat still through the entire show. When the show was over, he brought a towel from the bathroom and asked Edie to pin it around his neck just like Superman's cape. I was wondering if he wanted to go up on the roof. Would a bathroom towel work better than an umbrella?

He was running from room to room, jumping on and off the furniture, chasing Toby, yelling, "*Soup*erman! *Soup*erman to the rescue."

I guess he forgot about the lump of coal.

My mother put some Christmas albums on the record player, probably Perry Como. I was making sure the trains ran on time, carefully backing the freight cars into the siding to load or unload wooden barrels or gray plastic pipes. Ernie retired to the kitchen table, joining Edie, Norma, and Danny for some eggnog. Edie fortified hers with Cutty Sark. My father reminded her that it had already been spiked with bourbon, and as usual she showed my father her middle finger. My father asked her if she was certain that there was scotch in that Cutty bottle and not some of Nellie's vinegar. She showed him that finger again. Happy Holiday!

My father's sister, Aunt Kitty, called to wish us a Merry Christmas. I spoke briefly with my cousin Cathy and told her about my trains. My cousin Billy told me trains were for little kids, and he was getting a survival knife for Christmas, or at least he hoped he was, but what he actually wanted was a real hand grenade.

"Danny the Menace" was too busy saving Lois Lane to talk with his cousins. Then my Uncle Jimmy called to wish us a

116

Merry Christmas. Remembering the incident in Nellie's pantry years earlier, he too asked Edie if she was drinking actual Cutty Sark, and not vinegar. There were lots of comedians in my family in those days.

Some neighborhood kids came to the door, stood outside and sang a couple of Christmas carols. My mother gave them some of her Christmas cookies. I showed them my new train layout while Danny continued zooming around the house, cape flying, jumping from chair to chair. By that time, it was close to nine o'clock and Danny *Superman* was still flying, and beginning to wear on the adults in the kitchen.

My father decided it was time for *Superman* to retire for the night, told him Santa was watching and to avoid that lump of coal in his stocking he needed to go to bed very soon. Let's go. P.J. time. Actually, as I remember it, he was still sick with the Mumps, so he had been in his P.J.'s all day.

This all reached a quick and dramatic climax when he jumped off a chair near the train layout. He slipped and caught his chin on Ernie's white picket fence and the edge of the plywood, opening a large gash. There was a lot of blood in a very short time, soaking *Superman's* cape and leaving a small red stain along the edge of the cotton "snow" on the platform.

Danny started to wail. My father picked him up and ran to the kitchen sink, catching the blood in a towel. He held Danny while my mother, who was now on the first-aid squad but still taking training classes, began washing the blood away from the cut, although the blood kept coming. She held a towel against the cut and applied pressure.

There was no such thing as "911" in those days, so my father called our family doctor at home. Back then, family doctors made house calls, even on Christmas Eve. Doctor Carmine Pecora was not only our family doctor, he was also a friend of my father's. They often conversed in Italian. Several times over the years he had stitched up cuts that my father or his crew sustained. He also had delivered Danny, was treating his Mumps, and had sewn up some of his many cuts, usually the result of daredevil stunts. He was not surprised by the call, and he agreed to come and have a look at Danny's chin.

The injured *Superman* calmed down when he saw his old pal "Doc. P." arriving with his black bag.

"O Bambino Daniele, Cosa hai combinato ora, Eh?" asked Doc. P., adjusting his spectacles and gently removing the bloody towel from Danny's chin while my mother held him on her lap.

"What does that mean, what he said?" I asked my father.

"It means, 'What have you done now, Baby Dan?'"

That sounded reasonable to me.

"I was flying, like Superman," Danny said to Doctor Pecora.

"Yes, but it appears that it wasn't a good landing," said Doc. P. "Superman lands on his feet. No? Not on his chin, eh?"

The doctor peered through his spectacles at Danny's bloody chin. He removed instruments from his battered old leather bag. A little bit more crying, a little bit more blood, a pinch from the needle, several stitches, a big white bandage, a short cognac nightcap for kindly old Doc. P. and it was bedtime for *Bambino Daniele*.

118

My mother and father couldn't thank him enough for coming out on Christmas Eve. My father took out his wallet as he walked with him to his car. The old doctor waved it away, said *"Buon Natale,"* getting into his car.

"Felice Anno Nuovo," my father replied. Doctor Pecora waved and drove away. It was time for me to go to bed.

Danny (L) and Joe (R)

Christmas morning was memorable for several reasons. With his still swollen cheeks and a rather large white bandage on his chin, Danny looked like a vanilla Moon Pie with blue eyes. Next to the Christmas tree were two shiny Schwinn bikes, one medium size bike for me and a smaller version with training wheels for Danny. Some of my friends at school had been saying there was no such thing as Santa Claus, but at that moment I was pretty sure there was.

Danny (L), Joe (R)

The other great presents weren't from Santa Claus, they were from Edie and Ernie. There were two boxes that looked a lot like they would contain sweaters, wrapped in Edie's signature funny paper gift wrapping, with a big red ribbon around each box. My box contained a New York Yankees white flannel pinstriped uniform with a dark blue "7" on the back. Danny's box contained a white flannel New York Giants uniform with Willie Mays' "24" on the back. They were both a little big for us, but Ernie said that by summer we would grow into them.

My absolute favorite photo of us with Ernie was taken at the picnic table that summer in our backyard as he is showing me the proper grip on a baseball. Danny and I are wearing those uniforms. We both still have them.

A couple of days after Christmas while eating my breakfast, I asked my mother, "Is Pop Pop sick?" I had been hearing his cough and I was beginning to worry.

"What gave you that idea?"

She put down her coffee cup.

"I don't know," I said, pushing my scrambled eggs around on my plate, not looking at her.

"I've heard some of your conversations with Nana on the phone. It sounds like somebody's sick."

"Okay, Pop Pop *might* have something wrong with his lungs. That's why he coughs. You know when he was a ballplayer he smoked a lot, and the doctors think that might have something to do with it. Plus, there's always dust and lint in the air at the mill where he works."

"Is that why they want to do X-rays on Pop Pop?"

I knew that X-rays were serious. Danny had one when he was in the hospital.

"When are they going to do it?"

"They already did it. They found a small spot on his lung but it's nothing to worry about right now. They want to wait a while and do another X-ray. The doctor told him to quit smoking. He's trying his best. I promise from now on I'll let you know what's going on. For now, stop worrying about it."

But I couldn't.

Jack

Earlier, I mentioned collecting baseball cards as early as 1952. I collected cards through the late 1950s. Until that time, my friends and I were meticulous about our collections. Like most kids, we organized them by teams with a rubber band around each team. The American League teams in one Keds or P.F. Flyer sneakers box, and the National League teams in another, the boxes organized by each year.

I loved the Yankees. Tommy Reese was a Giants fan, and Jimmy Millwater, whose mother Miriam was in love with Duke Snider, was a Dodgers fan. Our respective collections reflected our allegiances. Ernie was a Phillies fan, but he was not a collector of baseball cards. He was pictured *on* a baseball card in his Braves uniform. I still have it.

In those days there was a nickel deposit on empty pop bottles (soda bottles to Jersey kids). Tommy, Jimmy and I attached our old Radio Flyer wagons to our bikes and we scoured the roadsides, alleys, and trash cans for empty bottles. Sometimes, never with permission, we would ride our bikes through the woods to a local trash dump, where we would hit pay dirt until the drunken old gatekeeper chased us. Wagons filled, we would pedal to the store, turn in the bottles and collect our bounty. We bought baseball cards, five or six in a pack, plus a flat piece of dried out bubble gum that tasted like cardboard.

At the end of our street, across from our laundromat baseball field there was a small building that housed two shops. There was Tony's Barber Shop, and next door a small store called the Sugar Barrel that sold candy, soft drinks, cigarettes, bread, etc. Two sweet old sisters, Gracie and Lydia ran the store. One of the ladies (and I can't remember which one but let's say Gracie) was a spinster, never married. Lydia was a widow with a disabled, wheelchair-bound son named Jack, who had cerebral palsy and who knows what else. His head was large and lolled to one side and he also drooled. I never knew exactly how old he was (someone told us he was around forty), but he was mostly bald with some spiky black hair sticking out from under the way-too-big-for-me Yankees cap that I gave him. It was almost too small for him, sitting pretty much on the top of his head, always crooked. In reality, it looked pretty goofy, but we always told him he looked great.

Jack rarely spoke except to utter certain sounds that passed for words. He actually came close to a few words from time to time, mostly curse words, but we understood him. He could barely raise his hands which usually rested in his lap. He had a sparse black beard that Lydia shaved from time to time. He also wore a colostomy bag that rested next to him on his chair. It was always covered by a cloth or hidden under his shirt. I asked my mother about it and she explained it to me in simple terms. Later, I learned first-hand and in great detail what an ordeal that must have been for Jack and his mother.

We loved Jack. He loved us in return, and his face lit up whenever we pulled up to the front porch of the store, our wagons filled with empty bottles. The rule at most stores was that bottles had to be clean or the storekeeper wouldn't take them. Gracie and Lydia didn't care because we were nice to Jack. They would even take bottles filled with mud, although we usually tried to wash most of the mud out. They also didn't count them. All they asked was that we haul them around to the back of the store and stack them in the empty wooden cases. Let the pick-up guys worry about any mud that might be in the bottles. Since they trusted us, we were studious about giving Gracie and Lydia a fair count.

Whatever money they paid us for the bottles went right back into the cash register to pay for packs of baseball cards, a nickel a pack. We would wheel Jack onto the porch, sit, and open our packs of cards. Jack got as excited as I did when I came up with a Mickey Mantle card.

"Hey Jack! I got a *Mickey Mantle!*"

He would utter something like, "Uh Huh! Uh Huh!" And something else like, "Nuh Semn."

He knew Mickey wore number seven. He would bob his big head up and down as much as he could, roll his eyes and laugh, his hands bouncing in his lap. We thought that was great. If Jimmy got a Duke Snider card, he would get the same reaction from Jack; same with Tommy and a Willie Mays card. If we were happy, Jack was happy. I knew that's why Gracie and Lydia didn't care if we brought muddy bottles to the store.

Of course, if I got a "Duke" or a "Willie" card and my pals got a "Mickey," we would barter; sometimes I had to throw in a Gil Hodges or a Roy Campanella card to get the Mantle. When we got cards we didn't want, guys like Wayne Terwilliger or Don Mossi, we attached them with clothes pins to the fender struts of our bikes to make motor noises on the spokes. We would also pin cards to the fenders of Jack's wheelchair so when we pushed him fast, the cards would make the same noise as they did on our bikes. He loved it when we pushed him fast, but I knew it made Gracie and Lydia nervous. But if Jack was having fun, they were okay with it. There was little fun or happiness in Jack's life and we knew that too.

Occasionally Ernie came to the store with us, or sometimes he would be there when we arrived with our wagonloads of treasure, buying cigarettes or a quart of milk for Edie. Gracie and Lydia used to flirt with him, and being the suave gentleman that I knew him to be, he flirted back, calling them "young ladies," but I'm pretty sure they were a lot older than he was.

Ernie was always kind to Jack, and it seemed as though he liked to sit with us on the porch while we opened our packs of cards. When one of us came up with a Phillies card, we gave it to Ernie. He made a big show of thanking us. Edie told me after Ernie died that she found a pile of Phillies cards in the drawer in his bedside table.

We also sometimes stuffed cards into Jack's shirt pocket. If it was a player he didn't like, he would let us know, getting a frown on his face and shaking his head. If we didn't like a certain player, Jack didn't like him either.

He drooled a lot when we gave him bubblegum, but he loved that too. We laughed when he tried to blow bubbles. I think he liked to see us laugh as much as we liked to see him laugh.

On the days when we played baseball on the laundromat field, we wheeled Jack across the street to watch us play. We would put a ball in his lap so he could throw out the first pitch. Usually, the ball dropped right next to the wheel chair, but sometimes one of us put the ball in his hand and guided his arm so he could throw it a little farther. Everyone made a big show of cheering for Jack. In return, he would bob his head and laugh.

At one of the games that Ernie, my father and I attended at Yankee Stadium my father offered to buy me a Yankees T-shirt. I talked him into buying one for Jack also. Edie sewed a big "7" on the back. Jack loved it. When we showed up at the store, most of the time Jack was wearing that Yankees shirt. Lydia said he wore it when he went to bed.

We would say, "Hey Jack. Lookin' *Good!*" He would bob his head and reply, "Nuh Semn." Jack wore that shirt to threads. I'm not sure Lydia ever washed it.

Gracie and Lydia were also understandably nervous when we brought Jack across the street to watch us play, and rightly so. If a foul ball hurtled toward Jack, he would have had no way to defend himself. We always stationed someone to protect Jack while waiting for his and on some days *her* next time at bat. Kathy McGee, a lefty, was a better hitter than several of the boys, plus she towered over most of us.

Full disclosure here, she was my first girlfriend and we used to play 'doctor' behind a hydrangea bush in my front yard. I think Jack had a crush on her as well. Kathy kissed him on the cheek once. It was simply another way for us to make his unfortunate life a little brighter.

One day, a teammate invited a kid from his class who lived in an adjacent neighborhood to come and play with us at the laundromat field. We jokingly called it Laundromat Stadium. The kid's name was Anthony Puccerella, and he was what my father called a punk. He had greasy black hair piled in a wave on top of his head that always reminded me of some kind of animal nest. He also smoked. None of us smoked, except maybe once or twice behind the laundromat, and it made me sick. Still does.

On this day, I was pitching. Tommy Reese was catching and Jack was alone in the cheering section, of course with someone standing by to deflect or catch foul balls. Anthony Puccerella came up to bat and said to Tommy, loud enough for the rest of us to hear, "How come yuz bring that gimp over here?"

Puccerella, supposedly a tough kid, was bigger than Tommy. Standing up slowly, Tommy removed his catcher's mask, carefully set it on the ground, came up quickly and threw a sharp right hook that landed squarely on Puccerella's face. Unlike in the movies, blood immediately spurted from Puccerella's nose.

I glanced over at Jack as we ran to keep this from going any farther, and he had a strange look on his face, part horror, part pleasure. Tommy slammed Anthony Puccerella to the ground, straddled his chest and proceeded to pummel the shit out of him until we pulled him off. Puccerella wiped his face with his shirt, picked up his glove and bat, got on his bike, gave us Edie's favorite middle finger as he rode away. We took him out of the line-up, cut him from the team and went back to our game.

Ernie sometimes came to watch us play, rarely offering advice unless someone asked for it. He sat on a cinder block bench next to Jack; with Ernie there we never worried about foul balls. The laundromat drained dirty water into the field behind the building, part of which would have been in left field, some in foul territory, the rest fair.

If you hit the ball into the muck out there two things happened. First, you were out. No discussion. Second, you had to retrieve the ball, which created a dilemma: either get your sneakers full of stinky green water, or wade into the ankle-deep quagmire barefoot, risking the onset of a common childhood malady called impetigo. With that in mind, we always tried to hit to center or right field. I don't think the EPA existed back then or the owners of the laundromat might have been in trouble.

Another major unwelcome feature and sometime impediment at Laundromat Stadium happened to be an abandoned giant concrete sewer pipe located a few feet from the foul line between home plate and third base. It was impossible to move it so we adjusted, but many third basemen sustained bruises chasing foul balls. The good thing about it was that we squeezed inside it during rain delays, especially if Kathy was playing that day.

We used to tease Jack, telling him we were going to wheel him into the muck in left field to retrieve the ball. He would frown, giving us the evil eye, saying something that sounded like, "Fuh Nuh! Fuh Ooo!" We knew what he meant.

Gracie and Lydia didn't talk like that. And woe to me if I ever used that kind of language and my mother heard it. The result would have been a mouthful of soap. I certainly heard enough profanity when I was around my father's crew, in the local bars and around the softball field where the men played.

When I did learn to talk like that, I had come by it honestly. The Marines might have had something to do with it as well.

I never did acquire a taste for Lifebuoy Soap.

Where's the Car?

I mentioned earlier that my father had been a pretty good athlete himself. He was a quarterback in high school and a second baseman on the baseball team. Never a professional like Ernie, he got his baseball 'fix' playing fast-pitch softball for a team called the Eagles, sponsored by *Whitey Eagleson Well Drilling*. "Whitey" was the manager and pitcher. They played games at night in a dusty, dimly lit old ballpark in the woods. At least it seemed that way to me; it wasn't quite the same as Yankee Stadium, Shibe Park, or Ebbets Field. There were only some splintery bleachers to sit on. Some people brought beach chairs.

The Eagles wore shiny red and gold uniforms and played against teams with names like *L&H Plumbing*, *Breton Woods Lumber*, and *Bevaqua's Esso*. Ernie and I sometimes went to watch and to cheer for my father. Most of the softball players who knew about Ernie were deferential toward him. After all, they were living out a dream playing softball while he had been the real thing, a big leaguer. I never heard him express disdain for softball as a lot of baseball players often do.

I liked to watch my father play. Ernie said he was scrappy, diving for balls, stealing bases. He was the kind of player you hate to play against, but love to have on your team.

When my father wasn't batting or playing in the field, I would get bored and wander over to a pond near the field to chase bullfrogs. As much as I loved him, my father wasn't Mickey Mantle, and Whitey Eagleson certainly wasn't Whitey

Ford. The teams usually went to the Red Lion for beers after the game. Most times I stayed home and hung out with Edie and Toby while Ernie went to the games. It was also a good chance to get away from my brother who was probably wrecking something of mine at the moment anyway.

One night Edie said she was in the mood for someone to serve her medicine to her, so she asked me if I wanted to go to Cucci's Bar with her. Cucci's had a shuffleboard game that I liked to play, so it sounded like a fine idea to me. The bar was also on the water so I could go out back and see if anyone was fishing off the dock.

"Okay. Let's go."

Ernie had driven his car, a '51 Chevy to my father's softball game, so Edie and I piled into her old '34 Ford with the rumble seat and were off for another adventure. It was a short drive to Cucci's and I sat in the front seat this time.

Dogs were allowed in the bar and sometimes wandered in and out. Looking back, I know they were cleaner and more well-mannered than some of the clientele. Edie told Toby he had to stay home this time and guard the house, but she said that she would tell his girlfriends at the bar that he couldn't make it tonight. As usual, Toby looked pissed off. I'm sure he was wishing he could say what Jack always tried to say to us when we teased him.

Edie knew everyone at the bar. Cucci's was a typical neighborhood bar, a lot like *Cheers*, only a lot rowdier and with less sophisticated patrons. Unlike *Cheers*, which might have had doctors, lawyers, or aspiring thespians as patrons, Cucci's had "Pineys," many named Gant, Gaskill, or Osborne.

I looked around for my father's "shit kickers," Harry and Jimmy, but they were either at my father's softball game or parked at the bar in the Red Lion.

Edie and I climbed up on bar stools between two Osbornes, Becky and Ed. Art Gant, cousin of my father's partner Randall, sat nearby. As usual, the bar was noisy, thick with blue haze, and smelling like beer and cigarette smoke. It was dimly lit in case some couples in search of romance decided to occupy a booth in the opposite corner from the shuffleboard table. There was a pool table at the other end of the room; there was always a crowd around it. Not so much at the shuffleboard game, so that's where I usually went. Like *Cheers*, most of the patrons knew Edie and me, and I knew most of their names. One of the women yelled, "Hey Edie, where's that handsome husband of yours?"

"He had another date; with his rowdy son-in-law!"

The woman laughed.

Like all good bartenders, Al Cucci knew all of the beverages of choice for his regulars. He produced a Cutty on the rocks for Edie and a Coke for me. Edie gave me a handful of nickels and I headed for the shuffleboard table in the corner.

From time to time someone came over and challenged me to a game, which was fine with me because they were generally drunk and I easily beat them. Most of the time, they left a few coins on the table before wandering back to the bar. After a while I got tired of playing shuffleboard. The smoke and noise were getting to me, so I wandered outside to see what was happening on the dock. Outside, two dogs whose owners were inside, wagged their tails and I felt bad because I didn't have treats for them. I patted their heads, wondering if they were Toby's girlfriends.

There were a couple of men sitting on the dock, sipping beers. Fish weren't biting but it was pleasant out there. Since I knew the fishermen, I sat near them for a while, petting the two dogs. The men asked me how my father was doing. The din from inside the bar was carrying outside and across the water. After a while the men packed up their fishing gear and walked to their cars. One went back into Cucci's followed by one of the dogs.

I went back inside and noticed that Edie and Art Gant were having a serious conversation. When she saw me, she shook hands with Art, gave Al Cucci some money, waved to some people at the bar and met me at the door. She was, as we always said, "feeling no pain," and I knew it. I was wondering if she would be sober enough to drive us home.

I didn't have long to wonder. We walked to, and *through* the parking lot to the road.

"Where are we going, Nana? The car is back there."

"Nah, let's walk."

She started to walk down the road.

"Walk? I don't want to walk. It's too far."

I probably stamped my foot.

"Nah, is a nice night. We can use the exercise."

And she kept walking.

I heard a car coming from the parking lot, so I turned and looked. I was surprised when I saw Art Gant driving Edie's Ford. He gave us a casual wave, drove slowly down the road in the opposite direction, the car weaving from one side of the road to the other.

"Nana, why is Art Gant driving our car?"

"Uh," she said, stopping and scratching her head. Her hair didn't look like a movie star's at that moment and she smelled like booze and cigarette smoke.

"I sort of sold it to him."

"But, why did you do that? I don't want to walk home. I'm not walking home."

"Up to you. I don't think the bus stops here."

She started to walk again. I had no choice but to follow her. It was about two miles from the bar to Edie and Ernie's house. I kept asking her why she sold the car to Art Gant and she said she would tell me tomorrow, and I wondered what Ernie would say. Edie held my hand, sobering up a bit as we walked. She kept telling me it was a beautiful night for a walk. There we were, two barflies walking home along the highway.

When we got home, she asked me to let Toby out and she went to her bedroom. I let him out for his late night sniff 'n pee, and together we went to my scratchy old couch bed on the porch. I thought briefly of going home to my own bed, just down the street, but decided against it. Ernie wasn't home yet; he was probably with my father and the rest of *Eagleson's Eagles* at the Red Lion, celebrating a win, or maybe a loss. It didn't matter, one way or the other they celebrated. I didn't hear him when he came home, but once again, I knew some shit would hit the fan in the morning.

It did.

Edie was still asleep when Toby and I went to the kitchen. Ernie was sitting at the table, sipping coffee and reading the paper. He was retired from Gibbs Underwear now, so he spent the summer "down the shore."

"Joey, Where's the car?"

"I'm not sure Pop Pop." I let Toby out.

"What do you mean you're not sure? *How did you get home*?" he asked, raising his voice, which he almost never did.

"We walked."

I really wanted some orange juice. "Did the Eagles win last night? Did Daddy get any hits?"

Ernie ignored my questions, setting his coffee cup and the newspaper down and pushing his chair back.

"*Walked*? *Why* did you walk?"

"Uh, because Art Gant was driving Nana's car."

"Well, okay, I guess Nana was feeling no pain, so she got Art to drive. But why didn't Art bring you home? Art doesn't have a license. And I'll bet he was drunk."

I was pretty sure Pop Pop was right. "Actually, he went the other way, down the road. He waved to us when he left."

Toby was scratching at the back door, having no further business to conduct and ready for breakfast, so I let him in.

About that time, Edie came into the kitchen, not looking wide awake. Toby was wagging his stub of a tail, surely thinking: chicken livers. Edie poured herself some coffee and sat down across from Ernie. Toby looked disappointed and sat down near his empty bowl, looking at it, then at Edie.

"Ede, where's your car?"

"Art Gant has it."

135

She looked at me. I shrugged. I didn't know any more about why Art Gant had the car than Toby did. I hoped she wasn't thinking that I would explain things to Ernie. I poured a glass of orange juice for myself from the pitcher on the table. Edie stirred her coffee.

"*Why* does *Art Gant* have *Your* car? And why the *hell* didn't he bring you home?"

"Well, I kind of sold it to him. Sort of. And he lives down the other way, you know, by the water."

"*WHAT*?" Ernie yelled. "What do you mean you *kind* of sold it to him? *Sort of*? What the hell's the matter with you? What the hell does that mean?"

He looked at me. I shrugged, sipped some orange juice, looked at Edie. I was pretty curious myself. Toby started to bark.

Edie looked at him, said, "Shut up."

Toby did, and sat back down by his empty bowl.

"One more time," Ernie said angrily. "What the hell did you do?"

"Well, we had a bet."

"A *bet*? What do you mean, a *bet*? About what? What the *hell* did you bet about?"

"Art bet me that he could chug a beer in less than four seconds, and I bet he couldn't. He did it in three seconds. Al Cucci timed him."

Ernie threw up his hands.

"That's a *stupid* bet. *Kids* bet on stupid stuff like that. And what the hell does that have to do with your car? Why does Art

Gant have your car? He doesn't even have a *damn* driver's license."

I had never seen Ernie this angry before.

"The bet was for fifty dollars."

"*Fifty* dollars?"

Ernie started to cough. We waited for him to finish. He pulled out his handkerchief and wiped his mouth. Sitting right next to him, I couldn't help but notice a spot of blood on the handkerchief. He quickly put it back in his pocket, but Edie had obviously seen it also.

"Ern, are you *okay*?"

"Don't '*Ern*' me, *Goddammit.*"

Ernie was very mad now.

"You bet *fifty dollars?* Where the hell did you get fifty dollars? And even if you *had* fifty dollars, why would you take it to Cucci's Bar? Are you *nuts?*"

Edie gave him a forlorn look.

"I didn't have fifty dollars. So, he said he'd settle for the car."

"Bull *SHIT!*"

He looked at me.

"Excuse me, Joey. I'm a little upset with your Nana right now."

I got that.

He stood up from the table.

"Edie, feed Toby."

He went outside, walked out to the street and looked toward our house, a few doors away. He came back in and said that my father's truck was still in our driveway, which meant he hadn't left for work yet; he asked me to go home to ask my father to pick him up on his way out. He told me that he and Nana weren't finished with their discussion, and he would see me later.

So, I walked home. My mother and father were finishing breakfast. I told them what had happened. My mother was upset when I told her the part about Nana and me having to walk home from Cucci's Bar because Art Gant was driving her car. I told my father that Pop Pop wanted him to pick him up on his way to work, I assumed to go to get Edie's car back.

My father chuckled, said he always thought Edie had a crush on Art Gant, handsome devil that he was, despite missing most of his teeth and rarely taking a bath. My mother gave him a dark look, but I knew she wasn't mad at him; she was mad at Edie. She certainly knew my father's irreverent sense of humor. (Now I know where I got mine.) He finished his coffee, put his red baseball hat on backwards, grabbed the keys to his truck and went to pick up Ernie to pay Art Gant a visit.

Later in the morning I went outside and checked Edie and Ernie's driveway. Her car was there. As it turned out, Art Gant remembered something about a bet with Edie but admitted he was pretty drunk when he left Cucci's. He also didn't remember how he got home. Art owned neither a car, a truck, nor a driver's license, having surrendered the latter to the state of New Jersey several years earlier after driving his truck off Cucci's dock, sinking the truck, two boats, and nearly himself.

Typically, without a sense of humor, the local cops were not amused, so Art Gant spent that night in jail, wet. Al Cucci bailed him out the next morning but not before Art gave up his license at the request of a judge who happened to like boats better than drunks. As a result, Art was quite used to walking home from Cucci's. He was rarely offered a ride, especially in the summer, considering his questionable hygiene.

My father related the details of the visit to Art's house at supper that night. He told us that Art had been wondering why Edie's old Ford was in front of his house in the morning, the left front tire resting partly atop a rusty lawn mower. The keys were still in the car. Ernie thanked Art for keeping Edie's car safe and told him the next time he was in Cucci's Bar he would buy him a beer.

My mother was still not happy about my late-night stroll with Edie on Mantoloking Road, but I knew she would get over it. I wasn't so sure that I would get over seeing the blood on Ernie's handkerchief, but it was still summer. There was still baseball at Laundromat Stadium, playing catch with Ernie, crabbing, the beach and baseball cards, as well as playing doctor with Kathy McGee behind the hydrangeas. I pretty much forgot about it.

Old Timers Day & Bob the Cop

Summer got a whole lot better when Ernie announced that he had tickets for Old Timers Day at Shibe Park for the following Saturday. I don't remember the exact date but I'm pretty sure the Phillies were playing against the Cubs. Ernie and I went to so many games in those days that it's hard to separate them. I think Curt Simmons was pitching for the Phillies in the regular game. My father and I drove to Philly, picked up Ernie and drove to the ballpark. The ushers at the park spoke to Ernie, saying it was great to see him, as always.

Prior to the regular game, there was a three-inning game featuring former players from as far back as the 1920s on up to the 1940s. Ernie knew many of them and one or two had been his teammates or he had played against them. Most of the old timers had played either for the A's or the Phillies, and lived in Philly or in the vicinity. Ernie had been invited to participate, but had declined the invitation. He told me he didn't want to make a fool of himself and that he was happy just to be there to see some old friends.

I told him I thought he was still pretty good. He chuckled and said he wasn't as good as he once was. My father told him he couldn't do any worse than some of these guys, many of whom were putting a lot of stress on the waistbands of their baseball pants. I was wishing that Ernie was out there on the field.

Most of the players, unfamiliar to current fans, were introduced to sporadic but polite cheers, most wearing old uniforms. Those from the early 1920s were of course, without numbers on their backs. Ernie pointed out some of the players that he knew, but I had only heard one or two of the names before.

They played a sloppy three-inning game with a few blooper hits, a lot of dropped balls and a lot of laughter. Many of the pitches barely reached home plate, and some of the younger players who had only been out of the big leagues for a few years hit the ball pretty well and could still run. They seemed to be taking the game a lot more seriously.

Truth be told, I was pretty bored, although those guys seemed to be having a great time. Ernie was smiling, and I knew he was re-living some of his moments in "The Show."

When the old timers waved to the crowd a final time and disappeared into the dugouts, the grounds crew came out, raking the field, smoothing out the infield and re-marking the lines around the batter's boxes. The public address announcer read off the starting line-ups for the Phillies and the Cubs.

During the first inning Ernie stood up and told us that he was going down to the clubhouse to visit with some of his buddies. I asked him if I could come with him, but he said not this time. My father winked at me and shook his head slightly. I understood. Besides, we had a ballgame to watch, and I needed to fill out my scorecard and keep score, as I usually did. Ernie was gone a long time. My father told me not to worry; he's probably having a great time with his old pals, going down memory lane.

Around the fifth inning, three old guys came weaving down the aisle toward where we were sitting. One of them was

Ernie. Thinking about it now, they were not that old. Actually, they were twenty years or so younger than I am now, and I still play baseball. I guess back then fifty was considered old.

They were certainly having a good time. I would have said "feeling no pain," but my father put it a little differently. He said they were "shit faced." They sat down in the empty seats near us and Ernie introduced his friends as Max Bishop and "Bullet" Joe Bush. Ernie said he had played against both of them and "Bullet" Joe actually struck him out once or twice.

"Couldin' hit my fastball," "Bullet" Joe said. "How ya doin' kid?"

He shook my hand, shook my father's hand. He had huge hands.

"Nice to meet ya."

He smelled like beer. They all did.

"You didn't get *me* out," said Max Bishop.

He looked at me. "Hi kid. You a ballplayer?"

He shook our hands.

"Padgett here told us you was a ballplayer. Yer gonna hafta grow some."

"Wait a minute Joe," Ernie said. "I got a couple of hits off you."

He looked around for the beer vendor. "How 'bout another beer?"

"Nah," said Max. "We gotta go. My daughter's waiting for us. She don't trust me to drive."

Some people sitting near us realized that these old guys were former ballplayers that they had watched earlier and asked them for their autographs. All three signed a couple of scorecards and the people went back to their seats. Max and Joe stood up, shook our hands again, and gave Ernie a hug.

"Good to see ya, Padgett. Get your ass in shape and play with us next year," said Max.

"Yeah," Ernie said. "Joe might be able to reach home plate by next year. You guys take care."

"Bullet" Joe Bush just chuckled. "Let's go Max," he said. "I'm getting thirsty, plus I gotta pee."

They waved and walked up the aisle. The fans with the autographed scorecards applauded. Max tipped his cap.

"I could use another beer," Ernie said.

"Are you sure, Ern?" my father asked.

I was glad my father was the one driving us back to Edie and Ernie's. My father would have never told Ernie that he might have had enough to drink, and he probably didn't want to deal with Edie if he brought him home drunk, which he already was. But Ernie had another beer and we watched the rest of the game. I don't remember who won.

When the game ended, we made our way to the parking lot. My father held the car door open for Ernie, who had a little trouble getting in, so my father helped him. I sat in the back. "Yep," I thought. "He's shit faced." I also thought that was a pretty cool expression. Ernie was waving to people in the parking lot. He leaned over and reached into his pocket, pulling out a baseball signed by most of the old timers who played in the game earlier, and handed it to me.

For some reason "Bullet" Joe Bush had signed his name in green ink. The only name I recognized was "Lefty" Gomez, who had pitched for the Yankees in the 1930s and 40s, and later was inducted into the Hall of Fame. I still don't know why he was invited to Old Timers Day in Philly. I thought maybe he struck a lot of those guys out. I still have that baseball but sadly most of the signatures are faded, illegible like so many of the autographed baseballs on the shelves in my studio. Later I asked Ernie to sign the ball for me. He did.

As we slowly followed the traffic out of the parking lot, Ernie continued waving to people, speaking to many of them. He kept saying, "Hi, how are ya? Nice to see ya!"

"Danny, you know you're my favorite son-in-law. Take us home."

"We're going. And Ern, I'm your only son-in-law."

"I knew that," said Ernie. "Whoa, look at that sweet thing in the blue dress!"

I looked.

"Pop Pop, she's fat!"

"More to love, my boy. More to love."

He waved to the fat lady in the blue dress. She smiled back at him. Ernie was definitely feeling no pain. Nana was also fat. I guess she had more to love.

"Hey Pop Pop, do you think she has a nice set?"

By then I knew what a set was. I didn't mention this to Ernie or my father, but Kathy McGee, my part-time nurse and part-time patient, was hoping to get a big set, and one day behind the hydrangea bush she showed me where her set would be when she got it. I said I'd like to see it when she finally got it, but I never did.

Ernie and my father laughed. Ernie settled back and the traffic began to thin out. My father looked back at me and winked. I realized at that moment how much I loved these two men. I knew that I was one lucky kid. I looked at my new baseball while Ernie appeared to be sleeping. My father asked me if I had fun tonight. I said it was great and I thanked him for bringing me along, and then it was quiet in the car.

Suddenly Ernie woke up and yelled, "Danny, *Pull over!*"

"What for, Ern? What's wrong?"

"I gotta take a leak real bad. Pull over right here."

"Ernie, you can't pee here. This is downtown Philly. We're on Broad Street for Chrissake. You'll get arrested. We'll all get arrested."

I thought about Yankee Stadium and the cop and my brother spitting on people.

"You want me to *Pee in your Car*?" Ernie yelled. "Pull over God Dammit!"

We pulled over at the next corner. I don't remember what the other street was but the sign on the lamp post next to a big green mailbox read *Broad Street*. Ernie slid out of the car, stumbled and put his left hand on the mailbox, stood swaying, unzipped his pants and proceeded to wet down the sidewalk, now holding on to the lamp post with his right hand. He looked over his shoulder at us, as if to say, "Look. No hands!" Swaying as he stood there, he leaned his head back, relaxing his shoulders, feeling better now, I assumed.

Cars were passing by in both directions. One driver honked his horn. A guy in another car yelled something as he went by. Ernie waved, still peeing, the stream now hitting the mailbox, while still holding on to the lamp post with his right hand, his left hand free for waving.

"I'm not believing this," my father said.

"Pop Pop sure had to pee!"

At that moment a uniformed cop came strolling around the corner, casually swinging a night stick, enjoying the peaceful evening. My father and I both saw the cop at the same time he spotted Ernie.

"Oh Shit," my father said. "This will *not* be good." He got out of the car.

"*Hey Buddy!*" the cop yelled. "What the *hell* are you *doing* there? You *can't piss here!*"

Ernie, still in mid-stream, still holding on to the lamp post, turned his head and looked at the cop who was moving toward him. Ernie squinted, still swaying a bit.

"That you, Bob?"

The cop stopped short and peered at Ernie.

"Oh, *Jesus H Christ. Mr. Padgett. Ernie!* I didn't recognize you. You *can't* be *doing* this. You *gotta* get *outa* here! I'm supposed to arrest you. *Jesus!* You can't *pee* here."

"I'm about done, Bob. I had to pee really bad. Hey Bob, how come you're not at the ballpark? I haven't seen you there in a while. Where you been?"

"I got transferred. I'm a beat cop now. *Please*, Mr. Padgett, put your pecker back in your pants, zip up and get the hell out of here. If my supervisor sees us, I'll be in a world of shit. Please!"

My father took Ernie's arm, leading him back to the car. "Sorry officer," he said, opening the door.

"Okay. Fine. Please, just get him the hell out of here!"

"Good to see ya, Bob," Ernie called out the window and waved.

"Yeah," Bob the cop said. "You too. But *please,* don't do this anymore. Not here anyway."

We drove away.

"That was my old friend, Bob the Cop. From the ballpark. He's a beat cop now. Used to be at the ballpark. Was nice to see him. How 'bout that shit! Should have introduced ya. Did I tell ya, I knew him from the ballpark?"

"Yeah, Ern, I got that. You wanna know something? If Bob had been a New York cop, Joey would be learning tonight about a whole other kind of set: *Handcuffs.* Ernie, you know, you are *truly* a *pisser* in every sense of the word and I love you. Can we go home now?"

Going to Milwaukee

A month before the start of the 1953 baseball season, the Boston Braves abruptly moved the franchise from Boston to Milwaukee's County Stadium. The National League office had to scramble to adjust the schedule. The Braves, now in a new home and enjoying a fresh start, completed their first successful season in several years. Under new manager Charlie Grimm, they finished in second place with a 92 and 62 record. Things were looking up for what had become a sad franchise in Boston.

Sometime during the fall of 1953 Charlie Grimm contacted Ernie to see if he would be interested in joining the Braves coaching staff for the 1954 season. While they had never been teammates, they had played against each other when Grimm played for the Pirates and the Cubs. I was unable to find out what their connection was, but one thing I did find out about Charlie Grimm was that he loved to have a good time, and he loved his beer. His nickname was "Jolly Cholly." The probable connection was Ernie's former teammate and good friend Johnny Cooney, who was also on the Braves coaching staff.

Whatever the connection was, it didn't matter to me. Pop Pop was going to be a coach in the major leagues for the Milwaukee Braves. I couldn't believe my good fortune. Ernie was already retired from Gibbs Underwear, therefore he was free to take the job, as long as Edie was okay with it.

I knew who most of the players on the Braves roster were; I had the baseball cards. The Braves had future Hall of Famers

Warren Spahn and Eddie Matthews, and in 1954 a promising rookie named Hank Aaron. They also had Joe Adcock, Del Crandall and Johnny Logan, three of my favorite non-Yankee players. Ernie and I had watched them play against the Phillies the previous year. I thought they wore very cool socks.

The thought of spending time with Ernie in Milwaukee, not to mention games in Philly and New York at Ebbets Field and the Polo Grounds, was so exciting that I couldn't sleep at night. I didn't know the details of a contract, the logistics, or anything else. I didn't care. I wondered what number Ernie would get, since there were no numbers on uniforms when he played. My pals at Laundromat Stadium would be jealous, but they would have to do without me for a good bit of the summer. I was going to Milwaukee with Ernie. I couldn't wait to tell Jack. I'd certainly be missing Kathy and her incipient set.

The dream came crashing down when Ernie went for a physical, which the Braves required. I think he knew even before the exam that he was getting sick. He had been coughing a lot more toward the end of the summer. Sometimes he cut short our throwing sessions, telling me he was sorry, but he was a little tired. He still came to watch us play at Laundromat Stadium, sitting next to Jack. Even those visits were less frequent.

Ernie thanked Charlie Grimm and the Braves for the offer; maybe next year. Deep down, I knew that wasn't going to happen. Goodbye Hank Aaron. I had seen more spots of blood on Ernie's handkerchief and as much as I tried, I couldn't get that out of my mind.

Christmas came and went. Ernie was pretty quiet most of the time although we did add another set of Lionel trains to the layout, a sleek *Burlington Northern* diesel and freight cars. Danny was as wild as ever and Edie had her old pal Cutty with her and she tried to cheer everyone up. It just wasn't the same. Ernie's physical exam and the results weren't mentioned, but the unspoken words hung heavily in the air. We knew that he had turned down Charlie Grimm's offer and I had a good idea why. Although I was disappointed, I was smart enough to not push the issue. I knew something was wrong.

The First Surgery

After Christmas, Edie, Ernie, and Toby went back to Philly. I concentrated on school or tried to, anyway. Normally, I would have been looking forward to spring training and the upcoming major league season, but I couldn't stop worrying about Pop Pop. What would I do without him?

I hadn't known about it, although I soon learned that Ernie had undergone what my mother told me was exploratory surgery on his lungs in Philly during the winter. Once again, I heard parts of the phone conversations about X-rays, and "Well, what did the doctor say?"

Sometimes I talked with Ernie on the phone. He said he was fine and he asked me if I was getting ready for spring training because we still needed to work on those short-hops, keeping my head down and my eye on the ball. I asked him if he really had an operation and he said it was no big deal. He told me to check on the *Norma Gloria,* and to make sure the tarp hadn't blown off. We were going to need a new can of caulk. He asked, as he always did, how Jack was doing. I said Jack was fine but he missed his pal Ernie. I did too.

Spring came. The Padgetts moved back "down the shore" and settled in. We caulked and painted the *Norma Gloria,* then put her in the water. We went crabbing again, ate breakfast at The Bazaar, and worked on my short-hops. Now Ernie was teaching me to bunt. I had gotten a little bigger and once in a while I hit a ball over the dirt berm that served as the center field fence at Laundromat Stadium. The berm also kept the dirty water in left field from seeping into the woods. Jack always cheered when I hit a dinger.

My father took us to Yankee Stadium a couple of times. We even brought Danny with us when he promised he wouldn't spit on anyone, but as my father joked years later, the only vendor who got past Danny was the beer guy. I never knew that a little kid could eat so many hot dogs and so much junk. He usually threw it all up from the open car window along the shoulder of the Garden State Parkway on the way home.

A few weeks before school was over for the year, my father and Ernie surprised me, showing up at the classroom door with Mr. Eid, the principal. We were going to Yankee Stadium for a night game. Mr. Eid made a big show "deciding" if he would let me out of school early. I was quite a celebrity that day.

The soda bottle business was good and our card collections were growing. I had a lot of Mickey Mantle cards. (Thank you again Mom, for throwing them all away.) There was even a rumor that our town would start up Little League Baseball the following summer. The bad news was that I might not be old enough to play. Ernie told me not to worry about it; he would make sure I played. He told me there was not another eight-year-old who could backhand a short-hop in the hole better than I could. I only needed to grow a bit. Kathy and I even opened the hydrangea bush doctor's office. Reluctantly, we let Gary Schmidt become an assistant. He was interested in Kathy's impending set also. It was a good summer.

Ernie still coughed a lot, and he would sometimes bend over and put his hand against his stomach or lower back. I saw more blood on his handkerchief, though he tried to hide it. One day, just before school started again while I was having breakfast, I couldn't stand it any longer. I had to know.

"Mom, is Pop Pop sick?"

"Why are you asking me that again?"

She had been standing at the sink, looking out the window. She sat down at the table while I poked at my cereal. I couldn't look at her.

"Yesterday he was coughing a lot and when he wiped his mouth, I saw some blood on his hankie. And that wasn't the first time. I think some of the guys saw it too but nobody said anything. I think even Jack noticed it."

"Okay, you'll find out sooner or later, so I might as well tell you. Pop Pop needs to have an operation on his lungs in a couple of weeks. He'll be in the hospital in Philly after the operation for a week or so. And then he'll be home. We'll go see him."

All of a sudden, I felt hot, then cold, that feeling you got when you were sent to the principal's office.

"Is Pop Pop going to die?" I asked. I was getting scared.

"What are they gonna do? Does he have cancer?"

I wasn't exactly sure what cancer was, but I knew it was bad.

My mother reached over and took my hand in hers. "Yes, if you want me to tell you the truth, I will. He has lung cancer. That's what they found last winter when they did the exploratory surgery. It was more than exploratory. They found what looked like cancer, so they cut it out and said they needed to wait and see if that took care of it. But evidently it didn't. New X-rays showed that he has a tumor on his lungs, that's like a lump that's very sore. They'll remove it. If they don't, it will get bigger which could be very bad."

"How?" How do they remove it?"

Now I was getting really scared.

"First they will give him something to make him sleep and they will make a small cut in his chest so they can look inside at his lung where the tumor is. Then they will carefully cut it out, sort of like you would do with a bad place on an apple that's otherwise good. He'll get a few stitches to close where they cut. You've seen stitches. Danny's had plenty of them. Remember that Christmas?"

I didn't care about that.

"And then he'll be okay and we can play ball again?"

"I'm sure you will. Your Pop Pop is a tough cookie. Like your dad, but in a different way. Now finish your breakfast. Pop Pop will be fine."

"I'm not hungry."

I pushed my cereal bowl away and bolted out the back door, running as fast as I could down the street to Edie and Ernie's. I was out of breath when I got there. They were just finishing breakfast. Toby was also eating and looked up from his bowl of chicken livers, wagged his stubby tail once, continued eating his breakfast. I wondered how he could eat that stuff because it smelled awful.

I had many things I wanted to ask but I didn't know how or where to start. Edie and Ernie could tell that I was upset.

Ernie came to my rescue. He stood up, said we needed to go down to the dock to check on the boat. I found out later that my mother had called to let them know she had told me about the surgery. In the car, Ernie told me it was a simple operation, one that the doctors did all the time and it had a lot to do with him smoking all the time when he was a ballplayer.

"But Pop Pop, why didn't you just chew tobacco like Ted Williams does? Instead of smoking?"

"Joey, I chewed tobacco, too. Almost all ballplayers did. And that's not good for you either. I want you to promise me that you'll never smoke."

Actually, I had already tried it behind the laundromat with my baseball buddies, but it made me dizzy. I didn't mention that to Ernie.

I had already picked up the habit of spitting a lot, like a lot of ballplayers did. We sometimes bought black licorice and stuffed it in our cheeks, and our spit came out a dark color like tobacco juice. My mother promised me that if I kept spitting all the time, I would develop a taste not so much for black licorice but for Lifebuoy soap. So now I couldn't spit, couldn't swear, and didn't *want* to smoke. What would my mother have done to me if she knew Kathy McGee and I played doctor behind the hydrangeas?

"Okay then, can I at least chew tobacco?"

I had never tasted it, but I learned later when we tried it behind the laundromat that it tastes terrible. It was nothing like black licorice, and it made most of us sick. A couple of the guys threw up after they swallowed the juice. We agreed that's probably why they spit.

"I don't think chewing is a good idea either Joey. You won't like it anyway."

I thought that was a pretty accurate assessment.

"Well, what about this operation?"

I wanted to know.

Ernie chuckled, reached over and rubbed my head.

"I'll be fine. A week in the hospital, a couple of weeks rest and we'll be throwing again. Don't you worry."

"You promise?"

"I promise. Anyway, we need to work on those short-hops if you're going to be a good infielder. You still turn your head sometimes, and we have to work on that. Not only that, but we're going to get you into the Little League next summer."

I wasn't real sure about that, but I could hope.

We bailed a few inches of rain water out of the Norma Gloria and headed home. Ernie said he wanted a cup of coffee so we stopped at our favorite greasy spoon, The Bazaar. When we sat down at the counter Sonny asked me if Ernie burned the eggs again. As usual, Ernie pointed at me.

That was in August. When September came, I went back to school and Edie, Ernie, and Toby went back to Philly. A week later, Ernie had his second of five major surgeries. In those days there was no such thing as chemotherapy, and radiation treatment was unproven and primitive at best. Surgery meant cutting out whatever looked suspect to the surgeons. Later I saw the scar from the incision in his chest. It wasn't small, as my mother said it would be.

The doctors removed the tumor and the prognosis was good. Ernie was in the hospital for about a week. A couple of days after he went home, my mother and I drove to Philly. An elderly Italian lady whom we called Aunt Stell, took care of Danny while we were in Philly. Aunt Stell took no prisoners, and Danny usually behaved himself when she was in charge. I think my father was afraid of her also. Like most old Italian women that I knew, Aunt Stell wore clunky black shoes and had a great mustache.

When we got there, Ernie was in bed, looking pale and tired, but he was glad to see us. So was Toby. Ernie asked me how school was going and if we were playing any ball at Laundromat Stadium. I said it was getting kind of chilly now, and we were playing football. He had a big bandage on his chest which I could see under his pajama top.

I sat next to the bed and we talked about baseball. The Giants had beaten the Indians in the '54 World Series. And how about that catch that Willie Mays made? Ernie said Tris Speaker would have easily made what has been called in baseball lore today "The Catch."

Ernie asked me how Jack was doing. I said Jack was fine, but he missed Pop Pop. All the guys did. I told him that Gracie and Lydia asked about him, and told me to wish him a speedy recovery. I guess they missed Ernie flirting with them.

Edie came upstairs and told me I needed to let Pop Pop rest a bit. Before I left the room, he said we'd be working on those short-hops in the spring and told me not to get hurt playing football.

I said that would be great and I would be careful. I looked back at him as I was leaving the room and his eyes were already closed. Edie said he was taking medicine for pain and it made him sleep a lot.

My mother and I drove home the next day. She was worried that Danny might set Aunt Stell's house on fire or lock her in a closet. I thought she'd probably lock *him* in a closet.

Ernie made a quick recovery. As my mother said, he was a tough cookie. The doctors said they were able to remove the entire tumor as well as some of the suspect tissue around it. Essentially, they had removed part of Ernie's lung, but the prognosis was good. As far as they could tell, the cancer was gone. They were right in part, but they were also wrong, which we found out soon enough.

A couple of weeks after Christmas, Ernie had a follow-up examination and some additional X-rays. C.T. scans and MRIs had not been invented yet. It appeared that Ernie's lungs were now cancer free, but he had been complaining of abdominal and lower back pain, along with, as Edie put it later, "having a lot of pain when he went to the bathroom."

He was examined by a team of specialists at Temple University Hospital. They concluded that Ernie had colon cancer, and he needed an operation as soon as possible.

That was early in 1955. Two weeks later, after finding extensive cancer, the surgeons removed a large section of Ernie's colon and bowel. Ernie came out of the hospital a couple of weeks after that with a colostomy bag attached to his side that he would wear for the rest of his life. Now Ernie and Jack had something in common besides a love of baseball. I wondered if this would be the end of baseball for Ernie and me. Happily, it wasn't.

The Tryout & The Trophy

The rumor about Little League Baseball became reality. There would be an inaugural season of the Brick Township Junior Sports League in 1955. That was the good news. The bad news for me was that the age bracket was nine through thirteen and a prospective player had to be nine years old by April 1st. I was eight, with my birthday coming up in July. Technically I didn't make the cut, but that didn't bother Ernie even a little bit. The tryouts were to be held on April 15.

Ernie made a slow but determined recovery from the colon surgery throughout the winter and early spring. He, Edie, and Toby had spent most of the winter in Philly. Ernie had begun stretching and walking, increasing the distances daily, and working on his stamina. Having been a ballplayer, he knew what it would take to get himself into some kind of shape. He was trying to become accustomed to his new companion, the colostomy bag, and the regimen it required. He had quit smoking for good, and the doctors told him he should slow down a bit on the beer, which he did. Now he used a cane when he walked, telling me his bad knee was bothering him. Deep down I knew it was more than that.

By the time the first tryouts were held, the Padgetts were back down the shore, and I got to see both my pals, Ernie and Toby, on a regular basis. Edie became more protective of Ernie, seemingly more serious and less fun-loving, but she still liked her cocktail hour. I thought she was treating Ernie a little bit like a baby but he seemed to be okay with it. I understand all that now also.

We weren't able to practice like we always had, so Ernie supervised while my father and I played catch. That was even more fun for me because my two favorite men were playing baseball with me. Ernie, as usual, stressed to my father that I needed to keep my head down on short-hops and ground balls. As a pretty good second baseman himself, my father agreed and proceeded to throw or sometimes hit hard grounders to me. I could move to my left and right, but the toughest ones for me were hard shots right at me, especially when they took a bad hop. *"Keep your head down!"* Ernie and Danny would yell at the same time. "There's a better chance of getting hit if you turn your head."

On tryout day, my father had a morning business appointment, so he dropped us off at the field and said he would return as soon as possible. He said that his appointment wouldn't take long. The field was basically an old softball field next to a chicken farm. When the wind was from the west, we got a good whiff of chickens, but it didn't exactly smell like Sonny's fried chicken at The Bazaar. The parking lot was full of cars and a lot of pickups. An older fat guy with a new red "Brick Township Jr. Sports League" hat, was scurrying around with a clipboard, writing down names, ages, desired positions, etc. Don't ask me how or why, but I still remember that his name was Joe Boland, the league commissioner.

There were other men, coaches I assumed, wearing similar hats, carrying bats and buckets of balls, organizing kids into groups around the field. There was a lot of chatter going on; it reminded me a little bit of batting practice at a big-league game. Parents stood on the sidelines or sat on the old green wooden bleachers, watching and sometimes yelling encouragement to their prospective big leaguers.

There were several lines of kids at each infield position, and four or five in each line. A tall, skinny, weathered looking guy wearing a blue hat with a 'Y' on it was hitting ground balls. He had a cigarette dangling from his lip that bobbed up and down when he spoke, telling the fielder whose turn it was to "Git *one*" which meant for the kids who didn't already know what to do by now that they should throw to first base after fielding the ball. That is *if* they fielded the ball. A good many balls were going through kids' legs into the outfield.

"Okay, git another one. Stay with 'er. Git in front of er. Git yer glove down," and so on, the coach was telling the kids, encouraging them. That coach's name was Emmet Gant. When I heard that, I wondered if he was related to Art or my father's partner, Randall. I figured he was since most Gants in our town were related. I was trying to remember if I ever saw him in Cucci's Bar. Edie would know.

Ernie and I stood by the backstop, watching, waiting to talk to Joe Boland. I was watching closely, wondering if these kids were any good, watching a gangly kid let a ball go through his legs, not getting his glove down. I thought, "Keep your head down dummy! Who the hell taught you to field a grounder like that? Certainly not Ernie."

I knew right away that some of these kids couldn't make the Laundromat Stadium team.

I looked around.

"Pop Pop, some of these kids are *big*."

I was getting nervous.

"Big doesn't mean good. You'll be fine."

Joe Boland walked up, sweaty and red-faced, carrying the clipboard. He looked closely at me. I was holding my glove and my bat. He shook hands with Ernie, still looking at me.

"He's not nine," he said to Ernie.

"He'll be nine in July."

"Not good enough. The rules say nine by April first." Joe Boland tapped his clipboard. "See, the rules are right here. We've got to go by the rules. He's pretty small anyway. What if we let him play and he gets hurt? Then it would be my ass in trouble for breaking the rules. I'm sorry."

He tapped his clipboard again and started to walk away.

Emmet Gant had been relieved of his hitting duties at home plate by another coach. He came around the backstop and stood next to Joe Boland, still carrying a bat, an unlit cigarette stuck to his lip. His hat was crooked on his head. It reminded me of the way Jack wore his Yankee hat. Evidently, he was Joe Boland's assistant.

He looked at me then looked at Ernie. "He ain't nine," he said.

He sure sounded like a Gant to me.

"Rules say a kid gotta be nine."

He put the cigarette in his shirt pocket, spit. I spit, as casually as I could, wishing I was a little bigger.

"I told them that," Joe Boland said. "I showed them the rules, right here."

He tapped the clipboard one more time.

"Bring him out next year." He walked away.

"Look," Ernie said to Emmet Gant. "I'll tell you what. Put him at second base and hit him a few grounders. If he doesn't look to you like he can play, we'll go home. Okay?"

Emmet Gant scratched his head. He put the cigarette back in his mouth; didn't light it. I was thinking, "Why doesn't he just chew tobacco if he's not going to light it?" Joe Boland was already talking with some other parents at the edge of the parking lot, clearly finished with us.

Emmet Gant looked toward the field, back at Ernie.

"Okay. Ain't makin' no promises. What's yer name kid?"

"Joe," Ernie answered before I could say anything. "His name is Joe."

"Okay Joe," Emmet said. "Trot yer ass out to second base and git in line with them other kids."

Ernie winked at me, said thanks to Emmet Gant.

"Don't thank me. He ain't made the team yet. Old Joe Boland over there ain't gonna like this."

I handed Ernie my bat and ran out onto the field; a real baseball field, a first for me. I had never been on a real field before, except for the field where my father played softball. I got in line behind four or five other kids. All of them were bigger than me. The biggest kid, who was in front of me turned around and asked me if my mama knew where I was. I wanted to tell him "Fuh Ooo," like Jack would have, but I didn't say anything to him. I was pretty nervous, so I casually spit.

When that big kid in front of me let three easy ground balls go through his legs, the fourth one taking a bad hop, hitting him in the chest, he didn't look quite as big to me. Actually, he looked like he might cry. He glanced at me. I looked straight back at him. I probably should have said something encouraging, but he had kind of pissed me off, so I looked down at the ground and spit again.

Finally, the coach hit an easy slow grounder to him. He fielded it clumsily and threw what we Laundromat Stadium veterans called a "lollipop" to first base that bounced several times and nearly stopped before it reached the first baseman.

"Okay, Good," said the coach. "Next."

Okay; my turn. I spit again, just for luck.

By now Emmet Gant was standing near home plate, watching the other coach hitting grounders to the infielders. Ernie was watching from behind the backstop, not far from home plate, leaning on my bat since he had left his cane in the truck. Joe Boland walked up and stood next to him. I wasn't paying attention to that. My heart felt like it was in my throat.

"I am not liking this," Joe Boland said to Ernie. "If he gets hurt, it'll be my ass."

"Just wait. Okay? He's not gonna get hurt."

I was up. I spit; tried to feel like a real ball player. I shook my shoulders; got loose. The coach hit a grounder to me, a fairly easy one. I fielded it, set my feet the way Ernie taught me, and snapped a perfect throw to first base, but the first baseman dropped it. Maybe he was expecting it to stop before it got to him like the big kid's throw.

"Let it go," I thought. "Don't throw it so hard."

164

Another coach who was watching, yelled, "Hey *kid*! That's not Gil Hodges over there. You don't have to knock him down."

I figured that coach was probably the first baseman's dad.

The coach at home plate hit another grounder to me, this one with a little more steam on it. I fielded it cleanly and threw to first, but I didn't throw it as hard as the previous one. The first baseman caught it, looking relieved.

I saw Emmet Gant and the other coach exchange looks. Emmet was leaning on his bat, the cigarette still unlit. They both looked at Joe Boland, standing next to Ernie behind the backstop. He looked back but didn't say anything, expressionless. The coach hit another hard grounder to me, this one really smoking. I fielded it and threw to first; no problem. I wasn't nervous anymore. I was doing what I had been doing for nearly four years. It was only me and my Marty Marion autograph model fielder's glove, perfectly oiled and nicely broken in. The only difference now was that I was on a real ball field that wasn't full of rocks, roots, dirty water from the laundromat and a ten-foot-long concrete sewer pipe next to the third base line. There was even real grass on the field.

"Hit one in the hole," Ernie told the coach.

He smacked it. This time I had to move quickly to my left, toward first base, diving for the ball. It landed cleanly in my webbing. I bounced once on my belly, jumped up, got my feet set under me, got my balance as Ernie had taught me, and made an accurate throw to first. He had taught me how important balance is, not only in baseball but in all sports. By now I realized a lot of activity had ceased and people were watching a little kid picking ground balls like a veteran. I was feeling better by the minute.

I looked over at Ernie and noticed my father was standing next to him. I didn't know when he had shown up. He saw me looking that way, and gave me a fist pump. Now I was nervous all over again since this was all happening quickly. I took a deep breath.

"Now hit one to his backhand side," Ernie said to the coach.

He did. It was a hard shot, but I was kind of expecting it. I got a good jump, went to my right and got my glove down, backhand. At the last second the ball took a funny hop; maybe it hit a rock or the grass lip on the infield. I had no time to think about it. Somehow, I kept my head down and my eye on the ball and it popped into my glove. I straightened up and threw to first. Pop Pop said sometimes it's better to be lucky than good. Like his triple play. I knew I had been lucky on that one. I looked at the coach at the plate, ready for another grounder.

Once again, Emmet Gant, the other coach and Joe Boland looked at each other. Commissioner Boland shrugged. I saw my father put his hand on Ernie's shoulder, suggesting they sit down on the front row of the bleachers behind home plate. Ernie said he was fine, but they sat down.

"Yeah, but can he hit?" Boland asked. "We haven't seen him hit yet."

"Yeah," Emmet agreed, looking at Ernie. "Can he hit?"

"Throw him a couple," Ernie said.

"Okay kid. Come on in here and git your bat."

The big kid who had been in front of me said, "Nice playing." I didn't answer him; that kid felt bad enough. I nodded and ran off the field.

Emmet Gant walked out to the pitcher's mound, carrying a bucket of baseballs. I handed my glove to Ernie, got my bat and walked to home plate. It was an actual real home plate; not a flattened trashcan lid, like at Laundromat Stadium. I stepped into the batter's box, tapping my bat on home plate. I would have knocked the dirt off my cleats like the big leaguers did, but I was wearing sneakers. I smoothed out the dirt in the batter's box, dug in with my back foot and spit.

"Kid, you gotta wear a helmet. Get the kid a helmet," one of the coaches said.

While someone was getting a batting helmet for me, I looked over at Ernie and my father, now sitting on the first row of the bleachers behind the backstop. Ernie winked at me and my father gave me a thumbs up. The helmet was too small for me and it pinched my ears.

"See the ball; hit the ball," Ernie always told me when we practiced. "Don't think too much."

"You don't have to kill it," my father always told me. "Just meet the ball."

Trying hard to remember those things when Emmet lobbed the first pitch, I swung and hit a weak dribbler back to him. He looked over at Joe Boland. I think my knees might have been shaking. So, I spit again and dug in, trying to look as badass as I could. The batting helmet was tight, still pinching my ears. I remembered more advice from Ernie, "Keep your head still," which wasn't easy, considering that my ears were being pinched and the helmet was squeezing my head.

I hit the next pitch which was a little bit outside between the second baseman and the first baseman. A clean base hit; not exactly smoked, but still a base hit. The next pitch I hit up the middle, slightly above Emmet's head. He probably should have caught it. A good pitcher would have; a good shortstop might have gotten it as well, but it was also still a hit.

The next pitch was inside, so I pulled my hands in toward my body the way Ernie taught me and I hit a soft liner over the third baseman's head, just out of his reach. Again, it wasn't a screaming line drive, but it would have been scored as a hit nevertheless. I then hit two soft bloopers. One was caught, the other dropped in just at the edge of the outfield grass. None of these balls were hit very hard, but I did put my bat on the ball and didn't miss a pitch.

"He ain't exactly killin' the ball," Emmet Gant said to the other coach who was standing behind home plate. That coach shrugged.

"Yeah. But he ain't missing any."

"Okay kid, last one." Emmet said. "Run this one out. Infielders, git ready. Throw him out at first base. Real baseball now."

I looked over at Ernie and he gave me our secret bunt sign: a hand on the belt buckle. Emmet wound up and threw the hardest pitch I had seen so far, but it was straight and over the plate. The other coach's comment must have pissed him off. I waited until the last second, squared up, and laid down a

168

perfect bunt between the pitcher and the third base line. I was on first base before anyone picked up the ball.

"The kid can run," said the other coach.

Emmet Gant looked over at Ernie, my father, and Joe Boland.

"Okay. He's nine," Emmet said, putting his cigarette back in his pocket.

Joe Boland nodded his head once, threw up his hands and walked away. A couple of the kids and a few parents cheered as I walked toward Ernie and my father, both standing now. They each gave me a hug. I felt great. I'm pretty sure Ernie felt better than I did. He was beaming, a proud Pop Pop. Now I knew why we had worked so hard.

"See, I knew you could do it. I'm very proud of you Joey."

"I am too," my father said. "All that hard work paid off, didn't it? Too bad Jack didn't see it."

I thought, "Too bad Kathy didn't."

My father held Ernie's arm as we walked to the parking lot. Ernie looked tired.

"Hey!" someone called from behind us. It was Emmet Gant, loping toward us.

"Ya did good kid. I'm putting you on my team, the Yankees. That okay with you?"

Now I knew what the 'Y' on his hat stood for.

It was more than okay. I would be on the Yankees! Maybe I would write to Mickey Mantle and tell him about it. I couldn't wait to tell Jack, Tommy, Jimmy, and Gary. And Kathy!

"Okay," Emmet said. "First team practice is next Saturday at Gordon Field in Shore Acres, 10 a.m. Y'all know where that is?"

My father said he did.

"I'll have hats n' a shirt for ya. Gotta git yer own britches. We lucky to git shirts n' hats. Maybe britches next year. You can wear sneaks or you can git some of them new baseball shoes with the rubber cleats on the bottom."

My father said we would do that.

Emmet turned to Ernie, "Mister Ernie, you want a coachin' job?"

"No thanks, I'll be in the cheering section. You'll do just fine."

"How 'bout you Dan?" Emmet said to my father. I realized then that they actually did know each other, probably from Cucci's or the Red Lion.

"I kin use a good coach. You still playin' for Whitey Eagleson's bunch?"

"I'll think about it, Emmet. See you at Gordon Field Saturday."

We headed for my father's truck. We piled into the old red *Gant and Seme* pickup. I sat in the middle while my father helped Ernie into the seat next to me. It smelled like creosote, cigarettes and beer in the truck. I didn't care; it was better than smelling the chicken farm next to the field. I held my bat and Ernie's cane between my knees.

"I'm hungry," my father said as we pulled out of the parking lot. "How about a couple of Sonny's grease burgers and some fries with a few cigarette ashes on them? What do you say Ern?"

"That's fine, Danny, and then I need a nap. Too much excitement for one morning, but damn well worth it."

He put his arm around my shoulders and squeezed my neck. My father was laughing, looking over at Ernie.

"You don't have to pee on a mailbox first, do ya Ern?"

"I'm good. Thanks anyway!"

We all laughed. I had a lot of good mornings with Ernie and my father, but this one ranks right at the top of the list, and I've never forgotten one moment of it.

Sonny was glad to see us. He was even wearing a clean apron. Some of the regulars asked me how my tryout went. I said it had been great; I was on the Yankees. Someone asked what number I got. I said we would get shirts and hats at practice next Saturday. I had no idea what number the coach would give me, and didn't care, as long as I got a shirt. Number seven was too much to hope for. Every kid wanted number seven, or "Nuh Semn," as Jack would say.

At practice the following Saturday, Emmet Gant gave me a blue hat with a 'Y' on it and the smallest shirt in the box, but it was still way too big for me.

Ernie said Edie or Norma could alter it so it would fit better. I didn't care. It was a blue Yankees jersey. The number on the back was "12," same as Gil McDougald. It wasn't Mickey Mantle's number, but I was okay with Gil's number. He also was an infielder like me.

With a few exceptions, there has been a "12" on the back of every baseball jersey I've ever worn, and I have worn many, playing for countless teams over many decades on the field, including the team I play for now. To all of my teammates, I am not Joe; I am simply "12." My best friend, Jim is "11." I sometimes wonder if someday, we'll forget each other's names.

Not only was I the smallest kid on the team, but I was also the smallest kid in the entire Brick Township Junior Sports League, 1955 inaugural season. A few of the thirteen-year-olds in the league weighed nearly twice as much as I did, and a few were nearly a foot taller. I may have had a great tryout, but my actual first season in Little League Baseball was hardly spectacular. Ernie kept telling me that big didn't necessarily mean good, but most of the pitchers were big *and* good, at least it seemed that way to me. Picture a 120-pound kid pitching to a kid who weighs 60 pounds.

I struck out a lot. Ernie told me I needed to stop swinging at bad pitches. Sometimes I still do, but I try not to. I'm not sure I even saw some of the pitches I flailed away at back then. An old baseball adage says, "Swing hard in case you hit it!" I tried to swing hard, but I rarely hit it.

The outfielders played me shallow, so if I did hit a blooper that would normally have been a hit, there was usually an outfielder there to catch it. Every once in a while, often surprising myself, I connected and got a clean base hit somewhere between the infielders who also played on the edge of the infield grass most of the time when I was at bat. No respect!

But I could run fast and I could bunt. I would look over at Ernie and he would put his hand on his belt buckle, our secret sign. I was able to wait until the last possible second to commit, and I sometimes got lucky, dropped down a bunt that didn't go foul, and I beat it out. The pitcher usually just glared at me.

What I did best at the plate, however, was walk. Ernie taught me to crouch low in the batter's box, and as short as I was, I had a pretty small strike zone which really frustrated the pitchers, most of whom weren't that accurate to begin with. Many of the older pitchers were already trying to throw curve balls, but most of the time the pitcher, and especially the catcher, didn't know where the ball was going.

When I did get to first base it was usually pretty easy to get to second on a passed ball. Occasionally, Emmet gave me the steal sign. Sometimes I made it; sometimes I didn't, but Ernie had taught me how to slide, so I did steal a few bases when I got on base. In truth, I wasn't on base that often.

I knew that Ernie's old timer drinking buddy, Max Bishop was probably right that night in Shibe Park when he told me, "Kid, yer gonna hafta grow some."

There were ten teams in the league, with fairly small rosters on each team, so I played a lot, always at second base, where I play even now as I'm writing this. If I had to move to my left or right to field a ball, I was fine. Balls that were hit extra hard and right at me caused me a lot of terror. Sometimes I had too much time to think, and I booted the ball. Sometimes I had no time to think, and I also booted the ball. I tried to keep my head down and my glove in front of me, like Ernie taught me, but some balls ended up going through my legs anyway. Hard grounders sometimes took bad hops at the last second. On the other hand, bouncing balls sometimes didn't bounce when they got to me, staying on the ground, scooting under my glove.

I would get so upset with myself that it almost made me sick, but Ernie told me not to worry about it because it happened to all infielders sooner or later. He told me that the best ballplayers have short memories and there would always be another game tomorrow. Don't dwell on mistakes; try to learn from them. Easier said than done.

Even today I would rather strike out three times in a game than make an error in the field. When I come home after a night game now, if I made an error in the field, I have trouble falling asleep.

I made some errors. Small consolation, but I wasn't the only one who did. Outfielders dropped routine fly balls, although in our league, fly balls were never 'routine.' First basemen dropped or missed throws; infielders and outfielders both made wild throws. We were kids, still learning and still being coached. But I always knew I was the luckiest kid. I had the best coaches in Ernie and my father.

By mid-summer, Ernie was having a lot of trouble walking and dealing with a lot of pain, but he refused to miss even one of my games. My father helped him walk to the bleachers behind the backstop or next to the dugout. He walked with a cane in one hand with my father holding his other arm.

At some point it became uncomfortable for him to sit on the hard benches in the grandstand, so my father carried a beach chair for him, setting it up next to the dugout. During the games when I wasn't on the field or on base, I would walk over to where he and my father were sitting. It seemed like he never got tired of telling me, "Keep your head down on those grounders." Even now it sticks in my brain.

I tried, but when a ball came screaming toward me it was hard to remember. In one game, a big lefty named Freddie Neuman was at bat, and somehow, I *knew* he was going to hit it to me, actually *at* me, which he did. It reached me in a split second, a 'grass cutter,' as we called it. I set myself and got my glove on the ground in front of me. If it stayed down, no problem; but it didn't. At the last second the ball took a wicked hop, bounced up and hit me squarely in the chest. I had no time to react. It knocked me backward and I landed on my back. It also knocked the wind out of me and for several seconds I couldn't catch my breath, which scared me.

Someone, maybe the shortstop, was yelling, "Get the ball! Get the ball! Cover second!"

I looked up, still trying to catch my breath, and saw Freddie Neuman digging for second, glancing at me as he went by.

The umpire yelled "Time out!"

Teammates and coaches came running. I was gulping air, trying hard to not cry. I almost made it, but when I saw my father running out onto the field, I lost it and started to cry. My chest hurt. Emmet Gant was helping me sit up.

The umpire said, "Kid, are you okay?"

"He's tough," Emmet told him. "He'll be fine. Come on, kid, shake it off. That's a helluva way to stop a grounder. Whyn't you use yer glove? At least ya kept yer chin outa the way."

I laughed, choking back tears, wiping snot on my glove. I looked over at Freddie Neuman, standing on second, arms folded, looking back at me.

"You son of a bitch."

"Hey, you shoulda caught it. It was right to ya."

I knew he was right; I should have. I looked around at my teammates, knew they were thinking, "Sure glad it wasn't *me!*"

"You okay Joey?" my father asked. "You want to come out of the game?"

"Yeah kid," Emmet Johnson said. "You wanna come out?"

"I'm fine," I said, wiping my nose again, this time on my shirt so I could take care of snot and any stray tears and not get it all over my glove. I looked over toward Ernie who was standing now, watching.

"Let's play ball," I said.

Emmet Gant clapped me on the back and headed back to the dugout. The rest of my teammates went back to their positions.

"You sure?" my father asked.

I said I was okay; I pounded my glove with my fist. "Yeah."

"Okay, Let's play!" the ump called.

I don't remember the rest of the game.

In Little League Baseball in 1955, there was no such thing as a participation trophy. Kids didn't automatically receive a trophy for simply showing up, as they do now. Trophies had to be earned. The players on the top three teams in the league were awarded trophies, the size of the trophy commensurate with order of finish. Kids on the first- place team received large trophies, second-place a little smaller, and the third-place team got the smallest. My team, the Yankees, finished in third place.

As far as I was concerned, my trophy could have been three feet high. It was actually about seven inches, but I could not have been prouder. To me, it might have been made of solid gold. There was a shiny batter, ready to hit, atop a base with a brass plate that read "Brick Township Junior Sports League Third Place 1955: Yankees." After the presentation ceremony during the league picnic, I walked over and handed it to Ernie.

"This is for you Pop Pop. Without you, I never would have gotten it."

He nodded and looked out at the lake next to the picnic area, I'm pretty sure to hide the tears in his eyes. I glanced over at Edie and my mother. They were both wiping their eyes. I would have bet that they were both thinking about the other Joe, the one who would have been a wonderful uncle to me. I looked at my father; he nodded and winked at me.

At that moment, I wished I had two trophies so I could have given one to my father, but he told me later that I did a very special thing when I gave it to Ernie. He also told me that he and I would have plenty of time to win many trophies together, which we did.

Ernie kept that trophy on the night table in his bedroom and on every night table in every hospital room he was confined to until the day he passed away. It's tarnished, but I still have that old trophy on a shelf in my studio next to Ernie's glove and his Cleveland hat.

A Brief Time at Angelo's

By the end of the summer, Ernie was weaker and no longer able to practice with me. He slept a lot, but mostly sat in a chair under the oak tree in the yard with Toby either close-by or on his lap. He rarely came to watch us play at Laundromat Stadium. With autumn and football season rolling in, as well as the beginning of a new school year, baseball was pretty much over for us. The sewer pipe next to the third base line stayed empty, except maybe for a stray cat seeking shelter from the rain. Baseball card collecting was over at least until spring, so we didn't see Jack as much as we did in the summer.

School started. I was in Mrs. Gettler's 4th grade class, but my heart wasn't in it. I couldn't stop thinking about Ernie being sick, that the time might be coming when he wouldn't be around anymore. Up until that time, I had been a good student, and I actually liked school, but that fall was different. I stopped paying attention in class, looking out the window a lot, worrying about Ernie and knowing deep down that I was going to lose him. When called upon, I often gave flippant answers, my classmates tittering. I became something of a class clown. I pushed my test papers aside, half finished; I flunked and didn't care. I skipped homework assignments, doodling at the desk in my room, drawing cartoon monsters or airplanes dueling in the sky. I spent a lot of time just pounding a baseball into the pocket of my glove.

One day, Mrs. Gettler kept me after class to try to find out what was bothering me, but I didn't want to talk about it.

Later, she called my mother, who had no idea (yet) that I wasn't doing well in school. She told Mrs. Gettler, whom I really liked and I felt sort of bad because I was upsetting her, what was going on with Ernie, but that was still no excuse for my behavior. Together, my mother and father laid down the law: Bad grades and bad behavior; no baseball in the spring. That got my attention, somewhat. Spring was a long way off, and Ernie was still sick.

I spent the weekend during the 1955 World Series in Philly, watching two games on TV with Ernie, and of course, with Toby in my lap. Edie was putting on a happy face; it was almost like the old days, but now the television screen was bigger. We watched those hated Dodgers beat the Yankees in seven games for their first World Series title in franchise history.

Several times during the games, I looked over at Ernie, only to see him asleep in his recliner. He also went to bed early, climbing the stairs slowly. Edie, Toby, and I watched television together, Edie saying that everything would be fine, that Ernie was just tired but would be ready for baseball season in the spring and was excited about watching me play.

Evidently, my mother had told Edie and Ernie about my bad behavior in school, so during that weekend visit Ernie told me how disappointed he was to hear about that. The *last* thing I ever wanted to do was disappoint him, so I promised him that I would try to do better.

A November appointment with his lung doctor followed by an exam indicated that his cancer was back. That meant surgery number five for Ernie and Christmas spent in the hospital again in Philly. This time they had to remove more of his lung. Some years later, my mother explained it. Back then they opened you up and they cut out anything that looked suspect. The doctors made no promises. Ernie's chest was a maze of angry looking pink scars.

I talked with Ernie on the phone two or three times a week when he was in the hospital and later when he was resting at home in Philly. We visited several times during the winter, and he seemed determined to recover in time for baseball and my second season in the Little League. It had now been re-configured into two divisions: 9 and 10 year olds in one; 11 through 13 in the other. That was great news to me. I was growing a bit, but I was still glad I wouldn't have to face those big 13 year old pitchers. I was pretty sure I could hit a 10 year old's pitching. Spring was coming; all I needed was for Ernie to get better.

While I started to work harder in school, doing my homework, not clowning around in class (as much), and taking my tests more seriously, away from school I began gravitating toward the "hoods," as my father called them. Technically, they were called juvenile delinquents.

Not far from our neighborhood, there was a grungy pizza parlor called "Angelo's Subs and Pizza," where, according to my mother, the bad kids congregated. She wasn't totally wrong. The pizza was pretty sour and smelled a lot like dirty feet, but there were two pool tables in the back room which was separated from the restaurant area by a two-section door, with the top half normally left open.

The pool tables were lorded over by our old nemesis from Laundromat Stadium, Anthony Puccerella and his older brother Paulie, along with Jimmy Basilotti, the owner's hoodlum son. Most of the pool players had long greasy hair, combed up in giant waves like Elvis. Brylcreem, "A Little Dab'll Do Ya," was well represented in those days. They were forever combing their hair, or their combs stuck out of their back pockets. Either Elvis or "doo wop" music played on the juke box, non-stop. The term for these would-be criminals in those days was "diddy boppers." They wore tight pants, pointed shoes, and turned their shirt collars up like Elvis. They all smoked, including a few nine-year-olds like me.

Angelo's was the first place the cops visited when someone reported a petty crime in town. The cops were on a first name basis with most of the clientele, and vice versa. I was forbidden to *ever* go to Angelo's. My father made it clear and simple, promising to whip my ass if he ever found me there, or heard that I had even walked past Angelo's.

Of course, I went there, knowing how risky it might be. I should have realized that my clothes always smelled like pizza, kitchen grease, and cigarette smoke when I came home. I guess that's how my mother figured it out.

On my first visit, I was with some non-baseball player kids from my class, who were well on their way to becoming junior hoodlums. They were also friends with the Puccerella brothers, which smoothed the way for me since I was the new guy. Anthony or "Pucci," who was now twelve, grudgingly acknowledged me, but couldn't resist asking how "Jack the Gimp" was doing and if I still hung out with that red-headed catcher who got lucky and beat the shit out of him a couple of summers ago. "Pucci" assured me that had Tommy Reese not sucker-punched him on the nose, he would have won that fight. Probably so, I agreed. Interestingly, I had always thought the same thing.

"Pucci" and I became friends, sort of. I think he thought of me as something of a project, taking me under his wing, teaching me the basics of how to be a hood. He taught me to smirk, but I could never quite curl my lip the way Elvis and the more accomplished hoodlums did. He taught me to play pool, smoke, and use expressions like "fugeddaboddit."

I didn't like smoking. I knew what it had done to Ernie; it also made me choke and get dizzy. I faked it, taking short, shallow drags, mostly holding the cigarette between my fingers like the cool guys did, or letting it dangle from my lip the way Emmet Gant and my father's "shit kickers" did while they worked. But that wasn't so great either; the smoke burned my eyes. Sometimes I thought about how disappointed Ernie would be if he knew I was hanging out at Angelo's and smoking, so I did feel a little bit guilty. I was having fun but deep down I knew I didn't belong there.

One gray afternoon in late winter I was leaning over the pool table lining up the eight ball, cigarette stuck to my lower lip, when I happened to look up. My mother was leaning casually on the half door to the pool room, watching me, perhaps waiting to see if I would sink the eight ball. She didn't look mad; she actually looked kind of amused. She didn't say a word, just calmly crooked her finger. *Come here.*

Oh Shit!

This was a *worse* feeling than the one you get when you're sent to the principal's office. For a brief moment, "Pucci" even looked scared, but he quickly recovered his composure and curled his lip. In that moment, I knew that my days as a prospective juvenile delinquent were over forever.

I laid the pool cue on the table, dropped my cigarette on the filthy floor and walked slowly toward Norma. She already had the lower half-door open. She reached down, grabbed my ear, twisted it a bit, and marched me through the restaurant, still not saying a word.

One of the guys said, "Bye, Joey."

Another one said, "Yeah, See ya around. Hey! You left the eight ball on the table."

And they all laughed. That was my last visit to Angelo's. A few years later, Jimmy Basilotti was busted for receiving stolen goods.

My immediate problem, however, would worsen considerably when the red *Gant and Seme* pick-up truck pulled into our driveway. My butt was already starting to sting in anticipation of Big Dan's belt. He came in as usual, smelling of cold, salty bay water, creosote, and beer. He hung up his red hat.

"Hi gang. Getting cold! As Yogi would say, 'Getting late early out there.' What's for supper?"

"Tuna casserole," my mother said. "Guess where your son was today?"

"Which one?" he said, taking off his jacket, kissing my mother on the cheek.

He was used to hearing bad things about Danny. He might have been up on a roof, walking through wet concrete on a new sidewalk, breaking windows, sliding across the thin ice on the river because another kid dared him to do it, or just poking around in someone's garage. What had he done now?

"Your *oldest* son. He was playing pool with those hoods in Angelo's back room. Not only that, he was smoking."

My father, often a bit impulsive, started removing his belt, always a bad sign. (Child abuse hadn't been legally defined back then.)

"What did I tell you about hanging out with the hoods?"

I looked at the floor.

"I'm sorry. I won't go there anymore. I just wanted to see what it was like."

My butt was already starting to sting, and the belt wasn't even all the way off.

"You're damn *right* you won't go there anymore. And in a few minutes, you won't be able to sit down either. Those punks are all gonna end up in jail. You want to go to jail?" The belt was off now.

"No," my mother said. "No hitting. Danny, put your belt back on. He'll be punished. I pulled him out of there by his ear. The embarrassment alone might be punishment enough."

"You did what?"

"I pulled him out of Angelo's by his ear," she said. "I'm sure he was embarrassed in front of all those juvenile delinquents."

"I was," I said, still looking at the floor, hoping for some sympathy.

My father laughed. I don't think he wanted to whip me anyway.

"Go to your room. We'll talk about it later."

He put his belt back on. My butt already felt better.

"No supper for him, either," my mother said.

"Aren't you gonna whip him?" my brother Danny wanted to know.

"You'd better mind your own business, Junior," my father said, sitting down, untying his boots.

"You should whip him! You'd whip me."

"That's because you usually deserve to be whipped. Nobody's getting whipped tonight. You're already a junior juvenile delinquent. So, you should quit while you're ahead. Go wash up for dinner. Joey, go to your room."

"No big deal," I thought, heading for my room. I didn't love tuna casserole anyway; at least I escaped Big Dan's belt.

I sat at the desk in my room, doodling, trying to draw a caricature of "Pucci", feeling like maybe I was home free, wondering about how Ernie was doing. I realized that I didn't like "Pucci" anyway. I guess he more or less simply fascinated me. Tommy Reese was right to have sucker-punched him. I picked up my Marty Marion autograph model fielder's glove, spit in the pocket, and rubbed it in. I loved that leather smell. Actually, I still do.

I looked at the posters of Mickey Mantle and Whitey Ford on the wall. Baseball season would start in a few weeks. I thought that maybe I should start behaving myself.

The phone rang in the kitchen, and I heard my father tell someone he would think about it. "Think about what?" I wondered. Probably someone wanted an estimate for a dock. I knew that if it had been Edie calling, my mother would have been on the phone, and even though she was mad at me, she would have let me speak with Ernie.

After dinner, my father came to my room, carrying a slice of apple pie on a plate. He closed the door and sat down on my bed.

"I thought you might be hungry."

"Thanks, Dad!"

I ate the pie in about three bites.

"I'm not crazy about tuna casserole either. But the pie is pretty good, isn't it?"

"Yeah," I said, around a mouthful of pie. "It sure is."

I assumed we were friends again, thinking now that I was completely off the hook.

"So, you're a smoker now, hey?"

He pulled a pack of Chesterfields and a book of matches out of his pocket.

"Not really. It makes me choke. I only did it to look cool."

"Yeah, I get that. You know, I always wanted to have a smoke with my oldest son. You're too young to drink. You don't drink yet do ya? I imagine some of those hoodlums drink. I can get us a couple of beers. What do you say?"

I thought of Edie and cocktail hour. Would tasting her gin and tonic count? "I don't drink."

"So!" my father continued. "Let's have a smoke together. Chesterfields okay? What's your brand of choice? I would figure you to be a Marlboro man, eh? I'm a Chesterfield guy myself."

He lit two cigarettes, unfiltered Chesterfields, and handed me one of them.

"I don't actually want to."

"Ah, come on. What's wrong with a father smoking with his oldest son?"

"But I'm only nine."

"I get that too, Joey. But as far as I know, you were nine at Angelo's today also. What's the difference? Come on, smoke away. Ah, nothing like a good smoke after dinner, eh?"

He blew smoke toward the ceiling.

"So, did you sink that eight ball?"

My mother must have told him I had been lining up the eight ball.

"No."

"Ah. Too bad. Maybe next time. Let's enjoy a smoke."

"Maybe *next* time?" I thought. "I don't think so."

I took a couple of tentative puffs; started to get a little dizzy. Chesterfields were strong.

"I don't want to smoke anymore."

I started to hand the cigarette back to him. Now, I was more than a little dizzy. At that moment, I knew this was not going to end well.

"Yeah, you do. Take a couple of good deep drags. Smoke like a man. Ya gotta love Chesterfields. A real man's smoke, eh? Come on, take a nice deep drag. Can you blow smoke rings?"

He blew a couple of perfect smoke rings toward the ceiling.

"I'll bet your buddies at Angelo's can blow great smoke rings."

I took a deeper drag, knew I was going to be sick; it was coming on fast. I was really dizzy now. My father reached down and picked up my waste basket, handed it to me. So much for the apple pie. My mother was outside the door, listening to me throwing up.

"Danny, is he okay? I think that's enough!"

"It's okay Norm, we're just having a nice father/son smoke. We're fine."

He leaned down close to me; I had my head in the waste basket.

"Jesus, you do look a little green right now. Damn good thing you didn't eat that tuna casserole."

I have never smoked another cigarette, and I never went back to Angelo's. When I saw "Pucci" or any of the other hoodlums in school, they either smirked or simply ignored me. One of them asked me if my ear had healed up, but after a few days they pretty much forgot about it and left me alone.

The Final Season

I had forgotten all about the phone call during which I heard my father tell someone that he would "think about it." He brought it up at breakfast the morning after our smoking party. I was still a little queasy, so my mother gave me some kind of tea. I didn't really want to go to school because I knew that by the time I got there everyone would know about my mother marching me out of Angelo's while twisting my ear.

"Chesterfield?" my father asked, tapping his shirt pocket. "A Chesterfield with morning coffee? Hard to beat."

"Not funny."

He squeezed my neck.

"How about some left-over tuna casserole? Norm, is there any left in the fridge?"

I curled my lip, my best "Pucci" impression. He laughed.

"I still think you shoulda whipped him," Little Danny said.

"And I still think you should mind your own business. The next whipping will probably be yours anyway."

Last night's phone call had been from Joe Boland, the commissioner of the Little League, the same Joe Boland who almost didn't allow me to play last season because I wasn't old enough. Joe had told my father that Emmet Gant would be managing a team in the older division in the re-configured league, and there were several openings for managers in the younger division, including the team that I had been assigned to. He asked my father if he would consider taking over the

189

team. That was when my father told him he would think about it.

He wanted to talk to me first.

"Oh Wow! That would be great! And maybe Pop Pop could be a coach!"

"Not so fast. We need to talk about your behavior first. You have to decide if you want to be a baseball player and a good student, or a hoodlum like your pals at Angelo's. You're gonna have to show your mother and me a whole new kid. The kid you used to be. This smart-ass attitude and bad behavior has got to stop, and your grades have to get better. And Pop Pop doesn't want to be associated with hoodlums. I'm pitching you the ball. Now *you* decide if you can hit it. What do you say?"

The thought of my father and Ernie managing and coaching a real team, not just the guys at Laundromat Stadium, was almost more than I could have even dreamed about.

"I promise! I will do better in school!"

"And no more smart mouth? No more back-talk to your mother? No more calls from Mrs. Gettler?"

"I promise! Please Dad, tell Mr. Boland you'll do it!"

My mind was racing. The queasy feeling in my stomach was gone. I no longer cared about being embarrassed in school. I would become a new kid.

"We'll see," my father said, finishing his coffee and getting up to leave for work. "Joe Boland told me to take a few days and get back to him. The first thing *you* better do when you get to school is apologize to Mrs. Gettler. We'll talk later. I've got to go to work. The bay water won't get any warmer. You can start by not missing the school bus."

"I still think you shoulda whipped him," my brother said.

Big Dan pointed his finger at Little Dan, then went out the door to his truck.

For a while, I did become a new kid. I made my bed, sort of. I took the garbage out without being asked. I put my dirty clothes in the hamper by the washing machine. I even volunteered to dry the dishes, since nobody had a dishwasher in those days. I even tried to be nice to my rotten brother.

The question in my mind was, of course, would Ernie recover enough from his latest surgery to at least be able to come to the games? There was no question that my father would take on the manager's job. I heard him talking with my mother about it a couple of nights later after I went to bed. She told him that my behavior was almost too good to be true, and when my father told me that Ernie wouldn't want to be associated with hoodlums, that was probably the game-winning hit. She could only hope that her dad, the tough old ballplayer, would be up for this.

A week later, my mother and I went to Philly for a visit, leaving my brother with Aunt Stell, the drill sergeant. Ernie was still tired, but he assured me that he would be ready for baseball season, maybe not actively practicing, but offering advice and helping my father.

Before we left Philly, Ernie and I sat in his basement workshop and had a long talk. He did most of the talking, explaining to me that he would never recover completely. He was still having a lot of difficulty breathing, and his "friend," as he called his colostomy bag, would always be with him, but he was doing his best to cope with it. He also told me that he already knew, and that I also needed to know that his doctors told him that his time with us would be limited. His cancer would probably keep coming back, and he did not want any more surgeries.

I had all I could do to keep from crying. He put his arm around me.

"But, I don't *want* you to die!"

"Listen to me. You and I have had a wonderful time together. When I lost your Uncle Joe, I thought my life was over. And for a while, I guess it was. It's a pain I hope you never have to go through.

"It hurts worse than cancer, operations, or anything else you can imagine. It's like getting beaned by a ninety-five mile per hour fastball when you're not wearing a helmet. Only it's worse; a bean ball can get you dead in a hurry. The pain of losing a child only makes you wish you were dead. I know you don't understand that now, and I truly hope you never have to."

Unfortunately, I had to, and I do.

He ran his hand through my hair, like he used to. I had been missing that a lot.

"Look. When you came along, I realized I had another chance. And I couldn't love you more than if you were my son. You being my grandson is about as good as it can get. I love you and I am so damned proud of you. *You* gave my life meaning again."

192

"I love you too, Pop Pop."

"Okay then, here's the deal. I know all about your bad behavior, the pool room, and other stuff."

I started to say something. He held up his hand.

"I'm not finished. As far as I'm concerned, that stuff is over. Fresh start; spring training and a new season. And I'm not only talking about baseball. You are going to do well in school from now on. You're going to help your mom, no more back talk, and be nice to your brother. I know that's hard sometimes. But you need to promise me. I don't want to hear any more bad stuff."

Nice to my brother? The one who wrecks all my stuff? That would be a tough one. But this is Ernie asking me.

"I promise."

"Okay. Then we don't need to discuss this anymore. Nana, Toby, and I will down there in a couple of weeks. I don't know about putting leaky old *Norma Gloria* in the water again. She might have made her last voyage, so we may have to buy our crabs at the fish market. But we'll get ready for baseball season. I'll help your dad as much as I can, but he doesn't need my help. Your dad is a good ballplayer and he knows baseball as well as anyone. He'll be fine as a manager."

"Does that mean he *is* going to be the manager?"

"Yes. He told me on the phone that he let Joe Boland know a few days ago."

"But you'll be there, right?"

"As much as I can. And Joey, this may well be *my* last season. You need to understand that. Let's make it a good one. Make us all proud, not just as a ballplayer, but as a person.

You'll have a lot more seasons. Okay? Let's go upstairs. Your mom's waiting. Now, help your old Pop Pop up."

In the 1950s, spring training games were not televised, so we listened to Mel Allen or Russ Hodges on our statically challenged old console radio on Saturdays, while watching snow pile up outside. As the great writer George Will wrote: "There are two seasons: Baseball season and the void."

We were definitely in the void. Snow and the ice on the river kept my father home from work, so my mother gave him a list of things that needed to be done around the house. Of course, I was recruited to participate, which was another test for the born-again "good son." I did my best to help out, avoided killing my brother and waited for the days to warm up, which they did in late March.

Laundromat Stadium was a sea of mud after the snow melted, so we played baseball in the street until my father had to pay some of the neighbors for several broken windows. Finally, the vacant lot and eventually the laundromat mud dried up and we were able to practice. It was great to see Jack again, although the new baseball cards weren't available yet. He was still wearing the now ratty Yankees shirt we gave him, although with a sweatshirt underneath. I asked him if he ever let Lydia wash it. He gave me his standard response, "Fuh Ooo." And he laughed his crazy laugh. We all laughed; it was great to hang out with Jack again. We wheeled him across the street to Laundromat Stadium and parked him close to the sewer pipe next to third base. Spring training was underway.

On warm afternoons, with the days getting longer now, I sat on the back steps, waiting for the old red truck to roll into the driveway. I already had my glove and Big Dan's glove ready. No matter how tired he was, my father would always spend fifteen or twenty minutes throwing with me. He was pretty good at throwing short-hops to my backhand side, the same way Ernie had done. I think of that a lot, and it always makes me smile because I knew that he worked very hard, but he was never too tired to spend time with me.

In mid-April, official Little League practice began at the field next to the chicken farm. The ambiance and fragrance had not improved during the winter, but nobody cared. Once again, our team was the Yankees. My father did not get to draft or pick his own players; they were assigned to the teams and the respective managers had to cobble together line-ups as well as they could. My father started with the basics, much like Emmet Gant had done the year before. He lined up prospective infielders and hit grounders. He hit soft fly balls to the outfielders. He had three rules: Always hustle. Know where you will throw the ball if it's hit to you. And *no* wild throws. He explained that this is a fun game, but like Ernie used to tell me, it's more fun when you play it right.

The toughest kid, Tommy Reese (Tommy, of Pucci/bloody nose fame) wanted to be the catcher, and that was fine with my father. Tommy didn't always catch the ball, but he was great at stopping the ball with his body. He was also fearless, and he was especially good at blocking the plate. If someone was tough enough to try to run over him, let him. Tommy was not afraid of anyone. He had a wide gap between his two front teeth and he could casually direct a stream of spit through the gap.

We thought that was pretty cool. The rest of us just spit the normal way. We still stuffed our mouths full of black licorice until one cheek bulged like big leaguers, and when we spit, it looked like real tobacco juice.

Donnie Hansen had the best arm, so my father put him at shortstop. I was the second baseman. Bobby Neuman, a cocky lefty who could catch anything that came near him was our first baseman. He was Freddie's little brother. Freddie was the kid who knocked me over with a wicked grounder last season and made me cry a little bit, which I was still embarrassed about. Our pitcher was a new kid named Mike Morgan, who was taller than everyone else and could throw pretty hard. A slight problem was that most of the time he didn't know where the ball was going when he threw it.

Tommy usually told the batter to be careful because even *he* didn't know where the ball was going. He blocked a lot of balls with his chest protector and shin guards, but Mike did manage to plunk a few batters. Tommy told them to shake it off. And *don't* rub it; you're a *sissy* if you rub it. And *whatever* you do, don't cry!

Most of the kids on the team had played baseball before, at least in their neighborhoods or on vacant lots as we had, but there were a couple who, in baseball vernacular, 'couldn't catch a cold.'

Louis D'Ambrosi was one of those kids. Louis' dad had been killed in Korea, and he lived with his mother, an older sister, and his ancient Italian grandmother. I don't remember her name but she reminded me of Aunt Stell.

Louis was a likeable kid, even smaller than me, with a dark complexion and bright white teeth, always smiling. He got the smallest uniform we had, but it was still way too big for him, as was his hat, which was always crooked and seemed to be held up by his ears. Hats in those days were not adjustable and were made smaller with safety pins.

Louis was always attentive, cocking his head and nodding seriously when my father showed him how to hold his glove and explained to him that he should never lunge at the ball. He told Louis that he needed to respect the ball but not be afraid of it; that's why he had a glove.

At bat, Louis was even worse. He was clearly afraid of the ball. My father worked patiently with him, lobbing pitch after pitch during batting practice, with Louis rarely making contact with the ball. My father kept pitching to him until he finally hit a couple. Through it all, Louis never stopped smiling; he was clearly happy to be on the team, a new experience for him, and he was trying his best.

Later, when Ernie was able to attend our practices, he tried to teach Louis how to stand in the batter's box, how to hold the bat, and to keep his eye on the ball. Louis would nod his head with a serious look on his face, and then go right back to his hapless style.

My father suggested to Ernie that maybe Louis could learn to bunt, but Ernie pointed out that Louis was afraid of the ball. He said if Louis tried to bunt and missed the ball, he ran a good risk of getting hit. His mother sometimes came to practice and she cheered when he made contact, even if it was a foul ball, embarrassing Louis. She thanked my father and

Ernie for their patience. She told them that Louis wore his uniform around the house and would have worn it to bed if she let him. In truth, I think she had a bit of a crush on my father, and I think Ernie had a crush on her.

He would say, "If I was thirty years younger..."

As I think about it now, she was kind of cute.

The rules said that everyone had to play at least two innings in the field, and everyone had to bat at least once in every game. My father was always a firm believer not only in the rules, but fairness in general, so Louis did get to play quite a bit, sometimes an entire game if we were short that night, usually in right field.

When he was out there, he stood as far away from home plate and as close to the outfield fence as he could so he wouldn't be tempted to try to catch a fly ball that might evade his glove and conk him on his head. It didn't matter that nobody in our division could hit a ball that far.

My father and the rest of us were constantly telling Louis to move closer to the infield, and he did move in, but slowly he inched his way back toward the fence. Because Mike was pretty wild, we couldn't tell him to try to keep the batters from hitting the ball to right field. The best we could do was hope that nobody did.

When Louis did get to bat, he usually struck out on three straight pitches, but once in a while he hit a weak ground ball back to the pitcher. During the entire season, he never made it safely to first base.

After our last practice, my father gave out shirts and hats. Would you believe he gave number "7" to Louis D'Ambrosi? Once again, I got number "12." Sixty years later, I still wear "12."

My father and Ernie got shirts without numbers. Ernie joked that he never had a number on the back of his shirt when he played in the majors, why should he get one now? There was one shirt left in the box, so I talked my father into letting me give it to Jack. It was also number-less.

When I gave it to Jack, he turned it over and looked at the empty back. He said, "Nuh Semn? Nuh?"

Sorry Jack. If I can't get number seven, you can't either.

Jack loved to come to our games. My father would lift Jack and his wheelchair into the back of the truck. Several of the kids on the team who lived in our neighborhood piled into the back of the truck with him. Ernie rode in the front seat with my father, who lifted Jack and his chair out of the truck at the field and parked him next to Ernie at the end of the dugout.

Our regular season began at the end of April, but Ernie already seemed to be running out of gas. He had been walking with a cane since the previous summer, and he was clearly in pain, and often had trouble breathing. Walking from my father's truck to the field, he usually had to pause a few times to catch his breath, and he still had a wracking cough. My father still brought a beach chair to the games so Ernie could sit at the end of the dugout with the team.

Once or twice, when I was spending the night with Edie and Ernie, while Toby and I slept on the porch, I overheard Edie telling Ernie that he didn't need to go to all the games because he needed to rest. He told her that pretty soon he would be resting for eternity, and he was not going to miss any of my games. End of discussion; Edie didn't push it.

By the end of the season, he was unable to walk on his own, so my father was lifting him out of the truck and literally carrying him to his chair next to the dugout, then going back to the truck to get Jack. Several times when I looked at Ernie, he was grimacing in pain, with one hand on his lower back.

Whenever our team was in the dugout, I sat at the end of the bench next to Ernie. When I was up at bat, I would look over at him and he would give me either the bunt sign or the sign to swing away. I still wasn't the greatest hitter in the league, but I did get on base a lot, either from walks or simply beating out ground balls in the infield because I was pretty fast. Ernie had taught me to not watch the ball if I hit a grounder to an infielder because I would lose a step running to first base; one step could easily mean the difference between an out and a base hit.

"Don't look. Just *run!*"

Once in a while I connected and got a legitimate base hit, and I did watch those. They always felt great; still do.

As the season continued, I started to hit better, with more confidence at the plate, not worrying too much about getting drilled by a pitcher who might be twice my size. Ernie had taught me that confidence at the plate played a big part in successful hitting.

I was having a good season, making few errors in the field, and I never got knocked down or had to wipe tears or snot off my glove. The most important thing was that Ernie was there, watching me. When I did get a clean base hit, I always looked

200

over at him and he gave me a fist pump or a thumbs-up. I don't know which one of us was proudest in those moments.

After every game, win or lose, my father treated the team to ice cream cones at the Dairy Queen, with most of the team, and of course, Jack, arriving in the back of the old red pick-up. Today, the cost of one small cone would be about the same as what my father spent on cones for the entire team; ten cents for a small cone, fifteen cents dipped in chocolate, a "Brown Derby."

We sat on picnic benches, teasing each other and reveling in the fact that we were real ballplayers, playing on a real field and wearing real and now dirty uniforms; the dirtier the better. I thought "How could life be more wonderful?"

That was until I thought about Ernie, sitting in the truck with my father, eating an ice cream cone on a warm summer evening. What were they talking about? Sometimes I would wonder what was going through his mind. Did he think about all those many celebrations he had participated in as a big leaguer? I doubt that they celebrated with ice cream cones; more likely it would have been beer, whiskey, and maybe a cigar.

Since the league had been re-configured, there were only six teams in our division now, and we were in a battle for first place. Mike had found a bit of a groove and was striking out more batters than he plunked. While we all made occasional errors in the field, the other teams did also, so the games could be high scoring affairs. My father jokingly called them "defensive battles."

Going into the last game of the season, we were tied with the Tigers for first place, with identical records. The winning team would be the league champion. Before the game, my father gathered the team around Ernie in his chair next to the dugout for something like a pep talk. He told us what a great season we had, that he was proud not only of the way we played, but more importantly, the way we had conducted ourselves. He told us to think of tonight's game as only another game. We had played the Tigers before, we had beaten them and we could do it again. He told us to play aggressive but smart baseball, but the main thing was to just go out there and have fun.

He asked Ernie if he wanted to say anything, but Ernie said he thought my father had said all that needed to be said, and he thanked us for letting him be part of the team. He held out his hand and we all put our hands on top of his.

"YANKEES!" we all shouted, more or less in unison.

"Okay," my father said. "Let's play ball. We're the home team; let's take the field."

He flipped the ball to Mike. "Go get 'em Mike. Keep it simple."

He sat down next to Ernie.

We ran onto the field, and first-baseman Bobby Neuman threw practice grounders to the infielders, while Mike threw his warm-up pitches to Tommy. Louis D'Ambrosi and another kid, Billy Gurski, were sitting on the bench in the dugout. My father told them they would both get to play. I'm sure that both of them were happy to sit on the bench and be enthusiastic cheerleaders.

I don't quite remember the details, but the lead went back and forth, both teams scoring a lot of runs on walks and errors, and a few hits. My father put Louis and Billy in the outfield for a few innings as he had promised. The rules were fairly lax in those days, so substitutes could rotate in and out of the game. Luckily, when he was in the game, Louis' peaceful time near the fence in right field was uninterrupted by fly balls, and I think everyone, including Louis, breathed a collective sigh of relief. He came off the field smiling, as usual. We all told Louis that he did a great job protecting the fence.

In the last inning, we were behind by two runs with two outs and the bases loaded. The tying run was on second base with the potential winning run on first base. A long single could tie the game, and I was due up next, already with two hits in the game.

The Tigers coach called timeout and walked out to the mound to talk with the pitcher, a big kid named Walter Sherwood, who threw pretty hard but he threw strikes, often right down the middle. I was swinging a bat in the on-deck circle; couldn't wait to bat.

My father called me back to the dugout. I thought he wanted to tell me something, some kind of advice.

"What?"

He turned toward the dugout. "Louis," he said. "Get your bat and your helmet."

"*What?*" I said. "You're kidding, right?"

"Joey, go sit down. Come on Louis. Get your bat."

I threw my bat down, ripped off my helmet and kicked it toward the dugout. I could not believe what was happening.

The game was on the line and I already had two hits. The home plate umpire removed his mask and took a step toward our dugout. There was little tolerance for bad behavior.

"It's okay, Jack," my father said to the umpire. "Pinch hitter. D'Ambrosi batting for Seme. Number seven for number twelve."

The umpire walked over to the Tigers dugout to advise the manager of the switch.

"Come on Louis, let's go. Joey, you go sit down. Louis, get a helmet."

I still couldn't believe it. Louis passed me, coming out of the dugout, dragging his bat.

"I'm sorry Joey," he said.

I glared at him. A pissed-off ten-year-old is without reason, compassion or humility. I kicked the dirt, spit and walked into the dugout.

"Come here, Louis," my father said.

He crouched down in front of Louis and put both hands on his shoulders.

"Listen Louis," he said. "I'm sorry I didn't get you an at-bat before now, but the rules say you have to bat at least once, so you have to. It's my fault but you can do this. You just go up there and do your best. Keep your eye on the ball and don't be afraid. You can do it."

"Coach, I don't want to. I'll strike out."

"You'll be fine, Louis. Just do your best."

Louis wasn't smiling now; he looked terrified. My father adjusted the helmet on Louis' head. In those days the helmets were basically padded leather earflaps with a pad in the back

204

and an elastic strap across the top of the batter's head with his forehead completely exposed.

"Go get 'em Louis."

Louis D'Ambrosi stepped into the batter's box, tapped his bat on home plate.

"Play Ball," the umpire called out.

I was in the dugout, still kicking anything close to me, not looking anywhere near Ernie. I knew I was behaving like a brat, couldn't stop. Nobody spoke to me. My teammates all started cheering, encouraging Louis, everyone except me. I knew he would strike out. I even hoped he would. It would serve my father right for taking me out of the game.

Walter Sherwood looked in at Louis, smirked, wound up and threw a fastball belt-high right down the middle, a hitter's pitch. Louis flailed at it and missed it by a foot. Strike one.

"Good *cut* Louis. Don't try to kill it. All you have to do is put your bat on it," my father called, clapping his hands a couple of times.

"Shit," I muttered.

Donnie Hansen looked at me and shrugged.

"Your dad knows what he's doing."

Sherwood wound up again and threw another fastball right down the middle. I was thinking I would have crushed that pitch. Louis waved at it and missed again. The ball was almost in the catcher's mitt by the time he swung the bat. Strike two. One more and the Tigers would be the champions.

From the stands behind home plate, Louis' mother yelled, *"We love you, Louis!"*

205

He glanced in her direction, tapped his bat on home plate. His eyes were wide with terror now. Sherwood looked toward the Tigers dugout, wound up and let fly another fastball, this one high and inside. Louis had no chance to hit it, and even worse, no chance to get out of the way. He barely turned his head. The ball smacked his leather helmet slightly above his left ear with a sharp crack. Louis went down, lying with his face in the dirt, not moving.

My father ran toward home plate. The Tigers manager and coaches came running. Players poured out of both dugouts and the Tiger players on the field ran toward home plate.

Walter Sherwood started screaming, "I'm sorry! I'm sorry! I didn't mean it! I'm sorry!"

Someone else yelled "Call an ambulance!"

I stayed in the dugout, still not looking at Ernie, but I knew he was looking at me. I could feel it.

There was a moment of terrifying silence. In the stands, all the parents and spectators were on their feet. And then, Louis slowly rolled over and sat up, tears in his eyes and dirt on his face, but smiling that beautiful smile.

"I don't need an ambulance," he said, wiping tears and dirt on his sleeve.

He looked at my father.

"I get to go to first base now, don't I? I get an RBI right?"

My father hugged him.

"Louis, you definitely get an RBI. You're also gonna have a nice purple knot on your head. You've got a hard head! I think the helmet cracked. Louis, you scared the hell out of us."

"Son, are you sure you're okay?" the umpire asked.

"Coach, maybe he should sit down for a while."

Louis stood up, wobbled a bit. My father steadied him.

"He's right Louis. Let's get you a pinch runner. You go sit in the dugout."

"No way, Coach. I'm going to first base!"

He jogged slowly to first base and smiled that beautiful smile through the tears and the dirt.

With today's rules and medical protocols, there is no way Louis would have been allowed to go to first base, especially in Little League Baseball. But he did. The spectators cheered; the players cheered. Louis stood smiling on first base, his one and only time that season.

"Okay," the umpire called. "Let's play ball."

With the bases still loaded, but our team still one run behind, Bobby Neuman stepped into the batter's box and promptly smacked the first pitch up the middle. Walter Sherwood somehow came up with the ball and threw to first base to end the game, making the Tigers the champions.

My teammates left the dugout and were gathering around my father. I stayed in the dugout.

Ernie spoke for the first time.

"Come over here."

My heart sank. I walked over and stood in front of him, head down.

"Is this the way your dad and I taught you to act?"

I could feel tears welling up.

"I'm sorry."

I looked down at the ground.

"Are you? You should be sorry. I'm ashamed of you acting like that. Haven't we talked to you enough about sportsmanship? Look at me when I'm talking to you."

"Yes."

I was fighting back tears, but couldn't.

"You obviously forgot whatever we taught you. I never *ever* thought I would see you behave like that. You don't understand this now, but some day you will. What your dad did today was about fairness, playing by the rules and about being a good sport. I knew a lot of guys who behaved like you have, and they lost the respect of their own teammates. If you don't have that, you don't have anything. It doesn't matter how good of a ballplayer you are. I am very disappointed."

Those words broke my heart. In my whole life, I never wanted to disappoint Ernie, and I had finally done that. I felt sick. I looked at Jack; he looked away.

"Hopefully, you'll learn something from this. If you don't, then I have failed, and your dad has failed, no matter how many short-hops you can pick. Now you get out there and congratulate the Tigers and you apologize to Louis and to the team for the way you behaved. I'm sure your dad will have something to say to you later. Now, as far as I'm concerned, this conversation is over. Tomorrow is a new day. Wipe your face."

I joined my teammates and we shook hands with all the happy Tiger players. I swallowed my pride and apologized to Louis. I knew I would be getting a lecture from my father when we got home, but he didn't say anything to me just then. He loaded Jack and his wheelchair into the back of his truck, helped Ernie walk on his own to the parking lot for the first time in several weeks, and the rest of us piled into the back of the truck as we had done all season. There was little to celebrate at the Dairy Queen, so we ate our ice cream cones quietly, wondering how the season went by so quickly.

At home later, my father told me he wasn't mad at me, but like Ernie, he was disappointed in the way I acted. He explained to me that what had happened was mostly his fault. Had Louis not batted in the game, the Tiger's manager could have protested the game and we would have forfeited, no matter the actual score. So, Louis had to bat.

"What if nobody noticed?"

"You know better than that. I noticed. Now go take a shower."

"Pop Pop is mad at me."

"No. He isn't. On the way home we talked about it. He thinks this was probably a good lesson for you, and you'll think about it for a long time."

I did, and I still do.

The Last Inning

By early September, Ernie was in so much pain that he could barely walk. Edie and my mother brought him back to Philly to see the doctors at Temple Hospital. Tests showed that cancer had invaded his spine, and they performed his sixth and final major surgery. The cancer was so extensive that Ernie ended up losing the use of his legs, and for the last few months of his life, he was confined to a hospital bed and a wheelchair.

Someone had given my father tickets to a Yankees game during the last week of the 1955 season. Normally, I would have been excited to be going to Yankee Stadium, but without Ernie it wouldn't be the same. I told my father to give the tickets to someone else, or take some of his pals to the game. I changed my mind when he told me about an idea that he had. We would try to talk to Casey Stengel, Ernie's old teammate, tell him what was going on with Ernie, and ask him if he could possibly send Ernie a note or a card to cheer him up. I thought that was a great idea, plus I might get to meet Casey.

While Ernie was still in the hospital, we went to Yankee Stadium. My brother wanted to come with us, so once again my father made him promise that he wouldn't spit on anyone. With the season nearly over, the Yankees were eight or nine games ahead of the second place Indians, easily coasting to the American League pennant and another World Series match-up with their long-time rivals, the Dodgers. On this day they would be playing against the hapless Tigers.

We arrived at Yankee Stadium early. Since we already had our tickets, we were in the front of the line when the gates opened. After an usher led us to our seats, he ceremoniously wiped them off with a mitt that looked like a dust mop. Then he casually held his hand out for the customary Yankee Stadium tip. My father handed him a couple of dollars and asked him where the Yankee offices were. The usher brought us to a long hallway that led to the offices.

After speaking with a receptionist, we were met by the team secretary, a dwarfish red-headed man who reminded me of a leprechaun. His name was Jackie Farrell, and he expressed skepticism when my father told him that he would like to speak to Casey. Of course, Farrell wanted to know why, and when my father explained the situation, Farrell said to come with him and he would see what he could do, with no promises.

"After all," Farrell said. "We're in the middle of a tight pennant race. Casey is pretty busy right now."

My father and I both knew that the Yankees were only one or two wins away from clinching the pennant in what had become a runaway.

"I understand," my father said, glancing at me as if to tell me to keep quiet.

"Okay," Farrell said. "Come with me. Once again, I make no promises."

He was carrying a clipboard. I didn't think I was going to like this guy Farrell very much.

We followed him down a hallway to an open door to the clubhouse. I could see blue sky and the top of the famous Yankee Stadium façade through what was obviously the dugout at the upper end of the slanted tunnel. Farrell told us to wait here while he went to talk to Casey.

Several players came out of the clubhouse, some carrying bats. I didn't recognize them. They nodded at us and walked up the ramp to the dugout, their cleats clacking on the concrete. We could see players getting dressed and chatting inside the open doorway. My brother Danny was peering around the door frame into the clubhouse, looking like he was ready to stroll right in.

"Danny, get away from that door," my father said. "Come over here."

Yogi Berra came out of the clubhouse, carrying two bats. *Yogi Berra!* I couldn't believe it.

"Hi Mr. Berra," I said.

I stuck my hand out. He wasn't as big as I expected him to be.

"Hey kid, how ya doin'?"

He shook my hand, looked at my father.

"Do I know you from somewhere? Yuz look familiar."

"I don't think so, Yogi," my father said.

"Yeah," Yogi said. "Yuz look familiar. Where ya from?"

"Near Point Pleasant," my father answered. "Down the shore."

"Yeah," Yogi said. "Nice down there. We got friends in Belmar. We go and visit them down there sometimes."

He shook hands with my father.

"Nice to see yuz," he said, shouldering his two bats. "Have a nice day. Enjoy the game."

He started up the ramp to the dugout, his cleats clattering on the concrete.

"Have a good game Mr. Berra," I called out.

Yogi waved and disappeared into the dugout. Jackie Farrell came scurrying out of the clubhouse, carrying a clipboard and some papers.

"Casey says he's sorry but he's too busy to talk to you today. Like I said, we're in a tight pennant race and he has a lot on his mind. If you'd like to write him a note, I can give it to him."

My father had already written a note with Ernie's contact information on it. He gave it to Farrell, who stuck it among the papers on the clipboard. Now I knew for sure that I didn't like Jackie Farrell.

"Okay," Farrell said. "I'll give it to him. Come on, I'll walk you out."

I don't remember anything about the game. I kept thinking that we had gotten what was called in those days, "the bum's rush." My father said it would probably have been easier to get into the White House to see the President. In my heart, I knew that Casey would not see that note.

Ernie never did hear from Casey Stengel, his former teammate, his friend. I was almost glad when the Yankees lost the World Series to the Dodgers in seven games. I hoped Casey would even get fired. Ernie was still in the hospital during the World Series, so I had little incentive to watch the games alone. In the 1950s, they played during the day, so except for the weekend games, I was always in school and usually saw only the last inning or two on our old black and white television when I got home.

After Ernie was released from the hospital, the Padgetts closed up their house in Philly, put it on the market and moved permanently to their cottage, down the street from us.

With my mother supervising Ernie's care, the small former guest bedroom became his world. The room included a hospital bed with an attached apparatus that enabled him to lift himself up and into the wheelchair. He rarely used it except to pull himself up to a sitting position, but mostly he just stared at the ceiling or watched television, barely paying attention.

My father had a carpenter friend come in and widen the door frames in the bedroom and bathroom to accommodate the wheelchair. Together, they constructed a ramp from the back door to an outdoor patio to enable Ernie to sit outside and enjoy the warm early autumn days. But unless Edie or my mother insisted on taking him outside, he stayed in the bedroom. The bed was too high for Toby to jump onto, so someone, usually Edie, lifted him up and he snuggled up and slept next to Ernie for hours at a time.

When I visited him, our conversations were strained, even though he seemed glad to see me. He looked very tired, and the twinkle in his blue eyes was gone. I was still embarrassed and worried that he was mad at me for the way I behaved in our last game back in the summer. More than that, I was worried that he was still disappointed in me.

The first and only time I summoned up the courage to ask him about it, he gave me that old Ernie chuckle and told me that he hadn't thought about it since that day, and he was never mad at me. He was pretty sure that I had learned a good lesson and he hoped that I had grown from it. He always told me that ballplayers had to have short but selective memories.

Then he asked me to give him a hug. This is a terrible thing to remember, but he needed a shave and he smelled sour. He used to smell like Old Spice aftershave. I thought maybe that was what being very sick smelled like.

The trophy that I had given him remained among the pill bottles, towels and rolls of medical tape on the night table next to the bed, the batter atop the trophy pedestal, still shiny, always ready to hit.

As the October days grew shorter, so too did our visits. Every day, I ran down the street to see Ernie as soon as I got off the school bus, not even stopping at home to drop off my books. I had to know that he was okay. I would retrieve the newspaper from the driveway and bring it into the house.

Edie had set up a card table on the porch where Toby and I used to sleep. She had photos, letters and other things spread out in front of her on the table. When I came in, she covered it all up. I asked her what she was doing and she said, "Puttering. Stuff. You know."

Then she would call out to Ernie, "Ern, the paper boy is here. I think he's a ballplayer buddy of yours."

If he didn't answer, she went into the bedroom to see if he was sleeping before she told me to go in.

"Hi Pop Pop. How are you feeling today?"

"I'm kind of tired today Joey. How are you?"

"I'm okay."

"How's school?"

"Boring," I said, reaching up and scratching Toby behind his ears. "I brought you the paper."

"Thanks. I'll read it later. How's Jack? Seen him lately? How about *Danny the Menace*? Still doing bad stuff?"

"Jack's fine, I guess. He said to tell you hello. At least I think that's what he said. Danny's still Danny. Still getting into trouble."

Sometimes I would tell him about some crazy stunt that Danny pulled, but then we ran out of things that seemed important enough to talk about, and I would start to fidget. Ernie would come to my rescue.

"Joey, why don't you go on home now? I'm kind of tired and I'm sure you have homework. I'll see you tomorrow."

"I love you Pop Pop."

I gave him a hug and patted Toby.

"I love you too Joey. Tell your dad I said hello, okay? Would you tell your Nana to come in here when she has a second?"

And that's how it went. I knew that time was running out for Ernie and me, and I couldn't do a damn thing about it. Life wasn't fair. I also knew that Edie and my parents were keeping things from me. I was still only ten-years-old, despite having smoked a cigarette with my father, shot pool at Angelo's, and played doctor with Kathy McGee behind the hydrangea bush.

Sometimes I heard parts of phone conversations while I was doing my homework, or sometimes in the middle of the night. Our house was small, so when the phone rang in the kitchen, we all heard it. Then I would hear my mother say, "Calm down. I'm coming down there right now. I'll clean it up. Don't try to move him. Just calm down, Mother."

She would run out the door and down the street to take care of some kind of problem with Ernie, usually with his colostomy, which seemed to constantly malfunction. She routinely had to perform some kind of procedure called "irrigation." I didn't know what that was, but it sounded pretty grim. Sometimes the colostomy connection came loose.

Several times my father had to go with her to carry Ernie from the bed to the bathtub while my mother would clean him up. Knowing Ernie as I did, I knew that he had to be embarrassed and humiliated, far more than I could ever have imagined at the time.

Edie was a tough cookie; we all knew that. This was a woman who joined the Army at forty three years old to replace her deceased son during the war because she felt it was her patriotic duty. But even tough old Edie was beginning to wear down under the strain.

Christmas came and went, but I remember only one thing about it. The project that Edie had been working on in secret at the card table on the porch was a lovingly crafted scrapbook detailing Ernie's life and career, as well as their lives together. It was her Christmas present to Ernie.

We were all gathered in the room with him on Christmas morning when Edie placed the box in her signature funny paper gift wrapping on Ernie's lap. Ernie cried like a baby when he opened it. We all did, except for my brother Danny who wanted to know why everyone was crying. I even saw my father casually wipe a tear from the corner of one eye.

I have never opened that marvelous scrapbook without thinking about that Christmas morning, standing at Ernie's bedside, watching tears roll down his cheeks.

The last few happy times that Ernie and I shared were when I sat with him, turning the pages and listening to stories he told me that I had never heard before, photographs reminding him of some of the crazy things he and his teammates did in the old days. If we had not had those sessions with the scrapbook, I wouldn't have known the stories or who most of the people in the old photos were, going back nearly one hundred years now. As I mentioned earlier in this book, Edie's scrapbook will always be one of my most-prized possessions.

Last Call

One bitterly cold morning in late February, while it was still dark outside, our phone rang. My mother was already up, in the kitchen making coffee and breakfast. She had told me it was time for me to get up to get ready for school, so I was getting dressed when the phone rang in the kitchen. I heard my mother yell, "Oh, *God No*! Calm down, Mother. Don't touch him! I'll be right there!"

My father had just come into the kitchen.

"What's wrong?"

"Daddy slashed his wrists!" she screamed, running for the door.

"Danny, call for the ambulance. Then come as fast as you can."

She ran out the door, grabbing her red jacket and white coveralls as she went.

I ran into the kitchen. My father was already on the phone, waving at me to be quiet while he gave the dispatcher the address at the Padgetts' cottage. Within a few seconds, while my father was putting on his boots, we could hear the siren in the tower above the Community First Aid Squad building about a mile away, wailing in the freezing darkness outside.

"What's wrong with Pop Pop? What did he *do*?" I screamed.

"I'll let you know. Nothing to worry about yet," he said, pulling on his heavy jacket, as he went out the door. "You stay here and keep an eye on Danny. I mean it! You stay here."

As he went out, Aunt Stell walked in. She lived across the street from us, and was always up earlier than anyone in the neighborhood. She happened to look out her kitchen window and saw my mother running down the street to Edie and Ernie's house. Good old Aunt Stell. I didn't hear all of what my father told her on his way out, but I did hear the word "suicide," and an icy chill ran through my body. Aunt Stell hugged me and told me everything would be alright.

"Is Little Danny still sleeping?" she asked.

"NO!" I screamed. "It won't! Ernie's gonna *die!* I don't *want* Ernie to die!"

"Honey we know that," Aunt Stell said. "And we don't know that he's going to die. Your mom will take care of him and the ambulance is on the way. I can hear the siren already. They'll get him to the hospital. I'm sure he'll be fine."

My brother Danny wandered into the kitchen in his pajamas, barefoot, rubbing his eyes. After his near-drowning incident a few years back, it seemed like he could sleep through anything. I was surprised to see him awake.

"Come here, Honey," Aunt Stell said, holding out her arms.

"Is Pop Pop sick again?" he asked.

He ran to Aunt Stell, and she hugged him. I saw my opportunity, and ran out the door, letting it slam behind me as I ran down the steps and out to the street. I could hear Aunt Stell at the door, calling to me to come back inside.

For only the second time in my life, I defied my father's orders. I didn't care.

"JOEY! You come back here!"

I had never heard Aunt Stell raise her voice before, but I kept running; didn't look back, realized I didn't have my jacket.

Pop Pop!

By the time I reached their house, the ambulance was already there. I had heard the siren, and had watched it turn the corner at the end of the street as I was running. Four white-clad figures ran toward the kitchen door, two of them carrying a wheeled stretcher up the steps, another carried something like a suitcase. The ambulance doors were open, red lights flashing in the early morning light. For a split second my mind flashed back to the day Danny almost drowned.

Curious neighbors, awakened by the siren, were standing by the fence, wearing bathrobes and winter coats over pajamas. I ran past the ambulance and through the yard.

Someone yelled, "Joey, what's going on? Is it Ernie?"

I kept running.

I remember thinking "Who else would it be?"

I ignored them, ran up the steps and into the tiny kitchen, for some reason it reminded me of crabs. Toby was barking. I saw bloody towels in the sink, blood spots on the floor. One of the rescue squad members, our old friend Tully Sittig, brought Edie out of the bedroom and into the kitchen, told her to sit down and please stay out of the bedroom so they could work. Edie was shaking and moaning. She was clearly terrified. Tully was patting her on the shoulder, trying to calm her down. Toby started growling at Tully. When Edie saw me, she told me to put Toby out on the porch, which I did, and came back into the kitchen. He continued barking.

Edie looked at me like she realized for the first time that I was there.

"Joey, Go Home!"

Tully looked at me; she also seemed to see me for the first time.

"Joey, you shouldn't be here. Why don't you go home? Everything will be okay. We'll take care of your Pop Pop."

I could hear loud talking in the bedroom: "Lift that... Put this... Just a second...Tourniquet ... Hang on Ernie."

Two more rescue squad members, both men, came up the steps and into the kitchen, carrying towels and blankets. They nodded at Tully and followed the noise into the tiny bedroom.

I heard my mother say, "Daddy can you hear me? Daddy?"

Then I heard my father say, "Come on Ern, you can do it. You've been through tougher stuff than this."

I had to get in there; had to know what was going on. Walt Sittig came out of the bedroom and saw me. Edie was still moaning. Toby was still barking on the porch. I was trying to sneak past Walt in the narrow hallway to get into the bedroom.

"Walt," Tully said. "Don't let him go in there."

Walt put his hand on my shoulder. I pushed it away, squeezing into the crowded bedroom between my mother and the two squad members who were raising the stretcher next to the bed. My father was on the other side of the bed with one arm behind Ernie.

An oxygen mask was on Ernie's face. His eyes were open but he was very pale. My mother was leaning over him, wrapping bandages around his wrists. She hadn't noticed me yet.

I had never seen or expected to see so much blood. The sheets under and around Ernie were soaked. There were bloody towels on the floor. I noticed a brassy smell in the room, learned later that's what blood smells like. When my father saw me between the two squad members, he looked surprised and then shot me a dark look that usually scared me, and I knew I was in trouble. Once again, I didn't care.

"Okay," my mother said. "I think we've mostly stopped the bleeding. Let's get him on the stretcher. Daddy, we're going to move you now. You stay with us now, you *hear* me? Stay with us. Danny, get his legs."

The two newly arrived men, along with my father carefully lifted Ernie onto the stretcher. Someone gently but firmly pulled me out of the way. Ernie groaned softly; at the same time my mother noticed me, staring at Ernie.

"Joey! What are you doing in here? How the hell did you get in here?"

"My fault, Norma," said Walt. "Sorry."

This time he didn't just put his hand on my shoulder; he put his hands under my arms, lifted me and carried me out of the bedroom into the kitchen and sat me down near Edie.

"Now you *stay* there," he said. "You were in the way."

Edie looked at me. "I thought I told you to go home?"

"I'm *not* going home yet Nana. Not 'til I know Pop Pop's okay."

"You know I love you Joey, but you're a pain in the ass sometimes."

For a brief moment, the old Edie that I knew and loved was back.

"I got it from you."

With my mother guiding the wheeled stretcher, they brought Ernie out of the bedroom, covered him with several blankets and someone held the kitchen door open. His eyes were closed.

I was sick with terror.

"Okay," my mother said. "Easy does it now. Be careful. Those steps are steep. Daddy, you stay with us now. You hear me? We're gonna get you to the hospital."

Edie stood up, leaned over Ernie, kissed him on his forehead and said "I love you, Ernie Padgett. Don't you dare die on me!"

At that moment, Ernie opened his eyes, turned his head slightly, glanced at Edie but looked right at me. He mumbled something, but the oxygen mask still covered his nose and mouth so I never knew what he said.

"I love you, Pop Pop."

I wanted to touch him. He closed his eyes and they carried him down the steps to the ambulance. I watched through the kitchen windows as several squad members and my mother climbed into the back, closing the door. I watched the red lights disappear around the corner at the end of our street and heard the siren.

My father spoke briefly to the neighbors and came back into the kitchen, carrying Toby.

"Get dressed Ede. I'll take you to the hospital."

She went to her bedroom.

"I'm coming, too," I said.

"No, you're not. You have to go to school. They don't let kids in the hospital anyway."

"I'm NOT going to school!" I yelled. "And besides, they do let kids in the waiting room."

"You know, Mister," he said wearily. "You are riding for a fall. I'm not very happy with you right now."

He began picking up bloody towels, rinsing some of the blood out and then putting them in the washing machine in the corner of the kitchen. He looked at me.

"Where's your jacket?"

"I forgot it."

"Go get it. Tell Aunt Stell I'll talk to her in a few minutes."

He went to Ernie's room for more bloody towels, and he stripped the bed.

"Then I can go with you?"

He looked at me and shook his head. "Why not? You might as well."

My father carried another armload to the washing machine and poured in detergent.

"If I say no, you're liable to show up at the hospital driving my truck. Go get your jacket and I'll come and get you in a couple of minutes. Edie, are you almost ready?"

He was emptying a can of dog food into Toby's bowl when I went out the door. He told Toby, "Sorry buddy, no chicken livers, plain old dog food today."

At the hospital, the doctor came out to the waiting room and told us that Ernie was alive but had lost a lot of blood. They were giving him a transfusion and it would be "touch and go" for a while. My mother came out to the waiting room, looking grim. She had blood on her sleeves and on the front of her white coveralls. She hugged Edie. My father put his arms around both of them. Edie was shaking. The other squad members were milling about. They brought coffee in paper cups to Edie and my parents.

My mother thanked them and said she would keep them posted, but they needed to take the ambulance back to the squad headquarters in case there were other emergencies. Tully hugged my mother and Edie. Walt shook hands with my father, pointed his finger at me.

"You know, your Nana is right. You *are* a pain in the ass! Norma, let us know if you need anything."

My mother nodded. "Thanks, I will."

I knew Walt was kidding, but I also knew that he was right. They left the four of us in the waiting room.

My mother looked at me. "Did you have any breakfast?"

I shook my head. My father brought me a dry doughnut and some hot chocolate from a vending machine. And we waited.

I never saw Ernie again.

They kept him in whatever they called the Intensive Care Unit in those days for nearly a week, where he remained in critical condition. Considering all of Ernie's other medical issues, the doctors decided that he could not be adequately cared for at home, and needed to remain in the hospital.

Within a few days, arrangements were made, and my mother and several squad members transported him to the Veterans Hospital in East Orange, New Jersey, where he died peacefully a month and a half later. My mother and Edie were at his bedside. He was buried next to his son Joe in the family plot in Philadelphia. Pop Pop was only 58-years-old. I never said good bye to him. I live with that.

I still mentally thank him whenever I backhand a short-hop up the middle.

There is a wonderful old joke that most baseball players have heard that goes something like this:

One old ballplayer is visiting a terminally ill teammate just before he dies.

The dying teammate asks his pal, "Do you suppose there's baseball in heaven?"

"What makes you think you're going to heaven?"

"You got a point. Okay, just for argument's sake, let's say I do go to heaven."

"Okay, so when you get there, if they have baseball, will you promise to let me know somehow?"

"I'll try."

A few days later, the sick ballplayer passes away and the few teammates who are still living show up for his funeral. (As Yogi Berra once said, "You need to go to other people's funerals, otherwise, they won't come to yours.")

A week or so after the funeral, the ghost of the dead ballplayer visits his buddy in the middle of the night, wearing a baseball uniform. His teammate sits up in bed.

"Is that YOU?"

"Yeah, it's me."

"How the hell did you get here?"

"Not important."

"Well, what's the report? Is there baseball in heaven?"

"Yeah well...I have good news and bad news. The good news is that there's baseball in heaven, lots of teams. There are games every day. The bad news is that you'll be starting at second base for the Cubs on Friday."

I truly believe there will be baseball in heaven. I also believe that my Pop Pop, Ernie Padgett, is the starting shortstop on one of the teams. The games never get rained out, and the season lasts forever.

Loose Ends

Edie

Edie outlived Ernie by nearly forty years, passing away at age 96. There were three more "Toby" dogs in her life before she died. My brothers, my sister Janine and I still joke about what a badass she was, never taking shit from anyone; while doling out plenty. If we needed something returned to a store, even under less than friendly circumstances, Edie was the "go-to" girl for the job. Sometimes she even returned things to a store other than the one where the original purchase was made. Few store clerks ever challenged her. Once when I accompanied her to a store, I heard a clerk say, "Here comes that old battle axe." If they only knew...

Big Dan

Big Dan, my father, died in 1999. We all signed a new baseball, and I put it in his hands before they closed the casket. I kissed him on his forehead; it was like kissing cold marble. There was standing room only in the church during his service, and a lot of funny stories were told.

A couple of years before he died, I was finally successful enough as an artist to do something nice for him. I treated him to a weekend on the Eastern Shore of Maryland, where I had shown my paintings for many years. We ate crab cakes and oyster stew; I showed him my favorite places along the back roads, old barns and boats that I had painted. I introduced him to some of my friends.

We attended three Oriole-Yankee games at Memorial Stadium in Baltimore. I even caught a foul ball that Reggie Jackson hit. My father thought that was great. He said the only thing he missed was my brother Danny spitting on the spectators. I have a photo of him in my studio that I shot at the last game when he didn't know that I was taking his picture. He is looking out toward center field. I still wonder what he was thinking, and I miss him every day.

Jack

A month or so after Ernie died, I gathered up some empty pop bottles to sell so I could buy some new baseball cards and I rode my bike to the Sugar Barrel. My heavy heart wasn't into collecting baseball cards then, but it was spring, there would be another baseball season, and I hadn't seen Jack in several months. I thought it would be fun to hang out with him for a while.

But the store was empty. There was a "For Rent" sign in the window. I went to the barber shop next door to ask Tony the barber what happened. He told me that Jack had a stroke sometime in the middle of the night in March, passing away the next morning. Gracie and Lydia closed up the store and moved to an assisted living facility. Tony didn't know where; somewhere in north Jersey, he said.

"That Jack," Tony said. "He sure was a pistol."

"Yes, he was. He was my friend and I loved him a lot."

Nuh Semn and Fuh Ooo!

"Hey," Tony said. "Sorry about Ernie. We'll all miss him."

"Yeah, me too."

Al Cucci

Al Cucci sold his bar, was elected mayor of our town, and remained in office for nearly 20 years, later becoming a powerful New Jersey politician. Having stood behind his bar for so many years and listening to conversations, I think he knew where a lot of bodies were buried. Figuratively, of course. Well... it was New Jersey.

Danny

"Danny the Menace" and I are still close. Instead of wrecking things later in life, he built things. He started out as the mountain manager at Snowshoe Ski Resort in West Virginia and ended up as president and general manager for nearly twenty years. He did, however, use a lot of dynamite when cutting the ski trails and the roads. I guess it was an inevitable step up from the firecrackers he used when he blew up my ship models.

While we are on opposite sides politically, we try not to go there. We talk about sports, or about the snakes and bears in his yard in Florida. I tell him about the snakes in my yard in North Carolina. He tells me about playing hockey. I tell him about baseball, and we bore the hell out of each other. I don't know anything about hockey; he hates baseball.

We compare our ever-growing litany of medical issues, still glad that we're both vertical. Like most brothers do, we frequently go down memory lane together. If I'm unable to remember someone's name or event, he can, and vice versa.

Sometimes I tell him he owes me for wrecking or blowing up all my ship models, but then he reminds me that I almost drowned him. So, I remind him of the time he jumped off the roof with an umbrella for a parachute, and he reminds me again of the time I got mad and chewed the top of my dresser. I guess we're pretty even.

Number Seven

Mickey Mantle and I became friends on a first-name basis in 1972 for about four days. It's a good story, but I'll save it for another time. Most of my teammates know it already, and can probably tell it better than I can.

Louis

In 1969, I was home on leave, having recently completed combat training in the Marines. I was attending a closed-casket visitation for a classmate and former high school teammate who had been killed in Vietnam. As I was leaving the funeral home, my old friend and former Little League teammate, Louis D'Ambrosi, now in the Navy, was coming up the steps. We were both in uniform.

Louis flashed that big beautiful smile of his. We shook hands, hugged each other, as fellow vets do.

"Did you ever learn how to hit a baseball?"

"Did you ever learn to control your temper?"

We chuckled.

"This is sad, isn't it?" he said. "I happened to be home and saw it in the paper. Carl and I were never actually friends, but I thought I'd pay my respects."

"Yeah," I said. "He won't be the last one either. A lot of our classmates are over there. Good to see you, Louis. If you go, be careful. If you get hit in the head over there, you won't be going to first base."

"I will. You too. I'll see you down the road."

He went up the steps.

"Hey Louis?"

He turned and looked back.

"How's your head?"

Louis smiled and went inside.

Kathy McGee

Kathy McGee, my first girlfriend and nurse/patient in our clinic behind the hydrangea bush did, in fact, end up with a great "set," as she promised me she would. Unfortunately, I never got to examine it. Kathy lives in Miami; we haven't seen each other in forty years but we still keep in contact. When we do correspond, she calls me "First Boyfriend." I call her "First Girlfriend."

Norma

Norma, my mother, passed away in 2016, in her 90s. Some years before she died, she decided that she wanted to learn to fly an airplane, so she went through training and earned her pilot's license. She also went back to school and ended up going from captain of the rescue squad to registered nurse, working in the same hospital that cared for both my brother and Ernie. As Edie did when she joined the Army, Norma felt that it was her duty.

On one of my last visits with her, she admitted to me that she used to stand at the bedroom window, which was slightly above the hydrangea bush. She would eavesdrop on the *clinic* below, holding her hand over her mouth to keep us from hearing her laughter. When she told me that, I thought, "Holy Shit! She pulled me out of Angelo's Pool Room by my ear. It's a damn good thing she never looked behind the hydrangea bush!"

One summer day, before my wife Sam passed away, we were in her happy place, her garden. While I was watering the hydrangeas, she asked me why I was smiling.

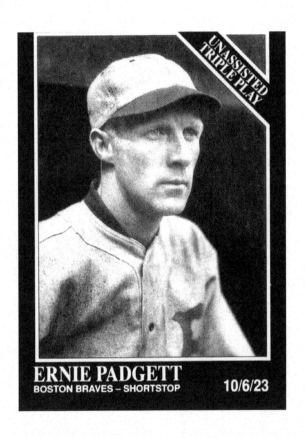

ERNIE PADGETT
BOSTON BRAVES – SHORTSTOP

UNASSISTED TRIPLE PLAY

10/6/23

Acknowledgments

Thank you, Edie, for the wonderful scrapbook which provided so much material for the book. The first part almost wrote itself.

Thanks to my brothers, David and Danny, for providing many great old family photos, some slightly damaged by Hurricane Sandy. Thanks especially to Danny for a wealth of subject matter. I honestly didn't try to drown you.

Thanks to Rhonda and Frank Amoroso at *simply francis publishing company.*

Thanks to friend and author, Anne Russell, who provided sound advice and encouragement.

Thanks to all my baseball buddies (those of you who can read) for all the enthusiasm. You know who you are. No freebies; you all have to buy the book unless you're a pitcher and you agree to throw me nothing but fastballs.

Special thanks to my long-time teammate and great friend, Jim Maresca, who did all the photo and technical work, and went above and beyond to make this come to fruition. Love ya, #11. I could not have done it without you.

More special thanks to my best friend, Anne Sutter; cheerleader, editor, backseat driver and provider of chocolate chip cookies. I *really* couldn't have done it without you.

Finally, thank you, Ernie. You are the reason I wrote this book.

About the Author

Joe Seme graduated from Florida State University in 1968 with a degree in English, and a focus on American Literature and Creative Writing. He was fortunate to have as a friend and mentor the Writer-in-Residence, Michael Shaara, who won the Pulitzer Prize for the classic Civil War novel *The Killer Angels*.

With the draft hanging over his head, in the fall of 1968 Joe moved to the North Carolina mountains, and worked in a ski shop, while writing short stories at night. One winter day at the post office he received two pieces of mail which would change his life. The first was a contract from a magazine to publish his first short story. The second piece of mail was a draft notice and orders to report for induction into the armed forces.

His plan was to enroll in graduate school after the hitch in the Marines, continue to write, and obtain a job teaching in college, but his brother Danny talked him into moving back to the mountains and opening a nightclub. He assured Joe that once the club got rolling, he would have time to kick back and write. It didn't work out that way.

To escape from the madhouse pace of the club business, Joe began painting for a diversion, mostly old barns and mountain landscapes, and a partner framed and hung some of his watercolors in the club. A chance encounter with the art critic for the New York Times in 1973 led to Joe's decision to paint full-time, and he never looked back. Writing, other than an occasional short story and several magazine articles, was put on hold, and a successful art career ensued.

Joe's paintings can be found in art collections both private and corporate, world-wide. His work has been featured on the covers of numerous magazines, in countless publications including *American Artist, Today's Art, Wildlife in North Carolina, Chesapeake Travel and Leisure, Ducks Unlimited* Magazine, *Town and Country, SALT* Magazine, and many others. He has been the Ducks Unlimited *Artist of the Year* in several states, and was a regular exhibitor in the prestigious Waterfowl Festival, in Easton, Maryland, where he was named "Artist of the Year" twice. He has had a retrospective museum exhibit, many one-person shows and participated in numerous group shows in museums and galleries around the country, winning numerous "Best in Show" awards.

Living next to a salt marsh teeming with wildlife in Wilmington, North Carolina, he continues to paint every day. Recently his dog portraits have become quite popular.

To order an autographed copy of ***A Short Season with Ernie***, to commission a dog portrait, to browse available paintings, prints or decoy carvings, go to www.joesemeart.com or email Joe at jseme@bellsouth.net.